The People's History

South Shields Scrapbook

by

John Carlson & Joyce Carlson

Members of Harton Methodist Church, Young Wives and Mothers' Club at their annual dinner in the Church Hall, July 1967.

Previous page: A children's snowball fight at Brinkburn, 1955.

Copyright © John Carlson & Joyce Carlson 2000

First published in 2000 by

The People's History Ltd
Suite 1
Byron House
Seaham Grange Business Park
Seaham
Co. Durham
SR7 0PY

ISBN 1 902527 70 4

Contents

A family group. A richly coloured carpet stretched across a clothes line partly masks the brickwork of their house in Florence Street. They are: Ted Bennett, George Bennett (aged $4^1/_2$), Irene Bennett (aged 2 years 9 months) and Sally Bennett (née Speller).

A vintage fire engine owned by Warden Newby. The location is likely to be the Claypath Lane/ Victoria Road area and the date mid 1950s. Mr Newby ran a road haulage business in the area and was also mayor of the town in 1970.

Introduction

This is the fourth book in a loosely-based series on South Shields, the others being *South Shields Voices*, *The People's History: South Shields* and *Images of South Shields*.

While putting together the first two books we sometimes had to struggle to find material. With the third it seemed to come in as an ever increasing torrent and by the time we called time we had more than a book and a half. A few months later we began putting together this book.

A large group of individuals are involved in selecting and sifting material for these books. Much of it has been originally gathered in the pursuit of hobbies, building up a family history or some kind of diary and, as a result, this book is really a kind of collective scrapbook.

The information accompanying the images has also been acquired from a variety of sources. Much came from conversations with the individuals who allowed us to use their photographs. After three years of going down to the Local History Library, on the E2 every time, some factual detail needed looking up and browsing through Hodgson's, *The Borough of South Shields* the authors have finally got around to buying their own copy. This work was printed in 1903 and is one of the definitive texts on the town. Other information comes courtesy of back issues of the *Shields Gazette*, *The Shieldsman* and numerous other trade and technical journals.

We would point out that a few of the images contained in this book are likely to be composite pictures or heavily airbrushed postcards. Almost a century before digital imaging, photographers were well versed in removing the unwanted and inserting the appropriate fictions.

The final book in this series is in preparation and the authors are always interested to hear from anyone who has either an interesting story or photograph concerning South Shields. In particular we would be interested in information concerning shops, pubs, transport and entertainment. We are can be contacted via the publishers. Several other people, some of whom have been involved with this series, are putting together other more specialist books on the town, possibly covering the local police force, transport and colliery bands. Again if you have any information on these topics please feel free to contact the publishers.

If you have any old photographs, documents or diaries there are several organisations that would be interested in taking copies including South Tyneside Local History Library in the Central Library, South Shields and the photographic archive of Beamish Museum. It is also interesting to see that sites devoted to the town are appearing on the World Wide Web. This development has allowed many ex-South Shields folk to keep in contact with their roots and in many cases make available to others photographs and momentoes that would otherwise stay stored away in draws thousands of miles away. If you are connected, typing in the search word Sanddancers should produce some interesting results.

A Women's Royal Army Cops recruiting drive. Patricia Headly is 2nd from left. The uniforms appear to represent a progression of those worn by members of the corps over time with the oldest example being towards the left.

ALL ALONG THE RIVER

TYNEMOUTH FROM THE GROIN, SOUTH SHIELDS.

Tugs wait off the buoys near The Groyne, *circa* 1910. The spelling on the postcard is incorrect. Hodgson notes that in October 1858 an enquiry was held at North Shields by the Royal Commission on Harbours of Refuge at which representative bodies from the district urged upon the government the claims of the Tyne as harbour of refuge. The commission later recognised much of the case and recommended that the government award a grant of a quarter of a million sterling towards the construction of the piers. Hodgson adds that as of 1900 that grant had never been given.

A group of South Shields River Pilots on the Lawe Top, *circa* 1920. Included are G.W. Purvis and George Wilson. Hodgson remarks that it is difficult to date the start of pilotage on the Tyne. It was confined to members of Trinity House, which was incorporated by charter of Henry VII, dated 5th October 1536, although the right seems to predate that. The Great Charter of James II, dated 1st July 1687, extended the jurisdiction of Newcastle Trinity House over the coast from Whitby to Holy Island. Trinity Brethren were relieved of the burden of bearing arms or serving on juries and exempted from impressment.

Another group of pilots. The office of pilot, however, was not to be specifically confined to Trinity House members which allowed Shieldsmen to exploit the town's natural geographical advantage for pilotage and the Lawe Top with its commanding view of the rivermouth was a natural place to set up residence. A practice of 'keeping the job in the family' also evolved, or at least amongst sons and direct relatives. A distinction was made between Shields 'Bar' Pilots who worked between the harbour and as far upriver as Whitehall Point and those who worked between Whitehall Point and Newcastle.

Pilotage was compulsory on foreign ships who were charged at a much higher rate than for British vessels. However, the 1824 Reciprocity Act gave foreign vessels the same terms as British ships provided their country's own ports gave British ships the same terms as native vessels. As compensation the British Government paid the full difference in both bar and river pilotage tolls to Newcastle Trinity House who were to pass it on to the pilots. But as many ships never went beyond Whitehall Point much of compensation went unclaimed. Newcastle Trinity House were supposed to put this surplus to the benefit of pilots, but Shields pilots believed they were being cheated of money rightfully theirs.

From 1861 the sea pilots were allowed to bring ships to the entrances of the Tyne and Northumberland docks which drastically cut the work available to the river pilots. Around that time the struggle over compensation seems to have come to a head. In a long legal struggle Shields pilots John Hutchinson and Robert Blair were deputised by their fellows to demand compensation in full from Trinity House at which point Trinity House stripped then of their pilots' licences. The next deputation consisted of well over a hundred Shieldsmen who refused to hand over their licences when asked. However, the 1862 Merchant Shipping Act allowed the Board of Trade to transfer pilotage jurisdiction to a representative body and the Tyne Pilotage Act created a commission of seventeen members, two of which were John Hutchinson and Robert Blair.

The Beacon public house. In the past the local of many a river pilot and today often a watering hole for many of those keen to get away from the Friday and Saturday evening hustle of King Street and Ocean Road. This view, probably late 1940s, shows the windows only semi-transparent, a common practice for many years. Whether it was to hide the drinkers from the world, or the world from the drinkers we are not sure.

Above: One of the most distinctive buildings in South Shields, the boathouse of the South Shields Voluntary Life Brigade. The date is *circa* 1900. It is likely several of the men outside the building are members of the brigade, the black shape on the ground seems to be a Standard Poodle. *Below*: Members of the brigade outside the clubhouse, *circa* 1910.

Members of the Brigade 'Going to Drill' outside the Pier Head Blockyard. The bravery shown by members over the years has been well chronicled by Boswell Whiticker in his book and here we present only a small account of a rescue after a gale hit the North East coast in October 1881:

'Hundreds of persons visited the South Pier last night, and after climbing over the heaps of sand which had gathered by the Coast Guard House, stood watching the drifting wreck, amidst showers of spray. Through the darkness, the schooner, fast going to pieces, could be seen bumping and rolling about as monstrous waves, white with foam leapt upon her. The members of the South Shields Brigade were still on duty in goodly numbers, lights were looked for, but none beyond those of the tugs and trawlers already mentioned were seen. At low water, just before midnight, the crew of the unfortunate vessel, assisted by some of the younger brigadesmen, boarded her by means of a ladder and brought ashore the bulk of the stores clothing and other effects. Excepting the captain and mate, the crew were all boys. Judging by their faces they seemed to think very lightly of their experiences of the day. As the night wore on the sky cleared and the moon shone out, illuminating the whole scene. The sea was yet enormously high and huge black walls of water, tinged on the surface with foam and spray continued to roll on the beach and the pier end. As the wind finally settled down to the west the brigade relinquished their watch at half past one.'

The J. Batey and Son steam tug *Francis Batey* towing a capsail schooner out of the Tyne. The tug was built in 1914 by Hepple and Co, South Shields, for the Batey company and named after their chairman. She was screw-driven by a 750 hp, 2 cycle compound steam engine capable of up to 12 knots. The Royal Navy acquired her during both world wars. During 1946 she was sunk and raised off Bill Quay. In 1920 she was transferred to the Lawson Batey Company, to Tyne Tugs in 1959 and the Blyth Tug Co in 1962.

Looking down the River Tyne, 1955. Brigham's Yard is to the right.

This and the series of photographs which follows detailing the construction of Brigham's Dock during the early to mid 1950s were taken by Roland 'Roley' Headly who worked on the dock as a bricklayer and was commissioned by the owners to record its construction. This photograph shows early excavations, 20th April 1954. A series of dates was given with each photograph which we believe to be correct.

Bracing for steel piling, 27th September 1954. The old Town Hall is visible to the rear of the picture.

A concrete batching plant, 9th October 1954. A narrow gauge locomotive used to move wagons containing concrete around the site is visible behind the lorry.

The dock head under construction, 21st May 1955.

The dock taking shape in May 1955.

A temporary concrete wall separates the dock from the river, 5th September 1955.

The workshops under construction, 26th August 1956.

The office block under construction, 26th August 1956.

The completed dock with keel blocks laid awaiting the first ship, 26th August 1956.

A ship in dock.

The Penny Ferry, South Shields

The Shields Steam Ferry, *circa* 1910. Although an invaluable link between North and South Shields, the service often seems to have attracted criticism and sometimes outright derision from local people. From 1856 this *Gazette* editorial provides a very sharp sketch of the service and an example of some of the searing criticism the paper could direct at those it felt were holding the town back.

'Twenty years ago there was an outcry against the inefficient accommodation afforded to the public of Shields by the steam ferry. Oxen and sheep and drays and kicking horses were crowded and crammed into the same ferry boat, with men women and children; and now despite the fact that the ferry company have had their investment more than amply repaid, oxen and sheep and drays and kicking horses are still crowded and crammed into this great thoroughfare between the towns! It is true that under strong pressure the ferries for beasts and human beings have been got to go every quarter instead of ever half hour between the towns and that additional ferries have been established at the New Quay and Penny Pie Stairs. But still the public is very indifferently accommodated. Had the thing been done by the Newcastle Corporation it would have been denounced as infamous; how much more indefensible the injury when it is inflicted by neighbour upon neighbour? We are determined to try to obtain something like the accommodation the public have a right to demand for the large tax they pay to the owners of the ferry company, and to this purpose mean to publish a list of shareholders with a view to showing the public whom they have to solicit for the requisite reform. A gentle continuous pressure exerted on the individual shareholders, a double share being exerted on Messrs Tinley and Lietch, the secretaries, some of which we mean to supply, would, we think, have a salutary effect. Why the Bishop of Durham should get fifty or sixty pounds per year for permitting the public to be crowded into nasty boats among cattle, sheep and dray horses, to their constant terror and not infrequent injury. There should be comfortable and commodious ferry boats, for passengers alone, running between the market places of the towns every five minutes with boats for cattle and carts every half hour. We shall return to this subject speedily and in the meantime ask our correspondents who are interested in the subject to state which facts have come to their knowledge regarding the dangers difficulties and delays dependent on the present clumsy system of communication between the twin towns.'

Almost everyone involved in the production of these books has realised at some time how photographs can be a 'generational thing'. This view from the former ferry landing stage looking towards Tyne Dock Engineering may well be unrecognisable to anyone under twenty. If it is the Alum House pub is just off the picture to the right. However, to many it brings back memories of walks down the gangway to the stage. If it was low tide the walk would be a steeply descending one and over the right hand side of the gangway there would be a view of evil looking grey black mud mingling with isolated and often oil streaked patches of water and skeletons of long abandoned boats. If it was high tide the walk would be much flatter but the water of the Tyne would often seem to be sucking and lapping around the stage with great force.

This slightly odd image shows a National Coal Board coal wagon being retrieved from the low staithes following an accident in the 1970s. The landing stage and the ferry the *Freda Cunnigham* can be seen behind.

NORTH EASTERN RAILWAY.

TYNE DOCK.

BIRD'S EYE VIEW SHOWING QUAYS, SIDINGS & STAITHS FOR THE SHIPMENT OF COAL BY GRAVITATION.

AREA OF DOCK. 50 ACRES.
7 MILLION TONS OF COAL PER ANNUM IS SHIPPED IN THIS DOCK.

Opposite page: An unusual bird's eye view of Tyne Dock and the surrounding area. The caption states it is an Isometrical Plan sent by the North Eastern Railway Company to the St Louis exhibition in 1904. This is possibly a painting taken from a series of aerial photographs. While researching this book we found a short description of the area prior to the commencement of the docks construction: '... from the corner of the Jarrow chemical works to East Jarrow there was nothing but a country road, skirted on one side by fields and on the other by Jarrow Slake, a part of which still remains at East Jarrow. At low water a wide expanse of mud was presented to view, while at spring tide the river spread itself over the pathway, rendering it impassable. There were no houses, save a cottage here and there, and the miners' dwellings at Temple Town pulled down some months ago. There was no railway station, the trains running from Shields to Jarrow without stopping. Indeed a good idea of the condition of this now prosperous part of South Shields may be formed by paying a visit to that part of the Jarrow Road which lies between Simonside and East Jarrow. All seemed a wilderness, there were no signs of activity, the country seemed forsaken.'

A photograph from an advertisement for C.R. Toomer and Co. The picture gives an unusual view of Tyne Dock, the entrance to which is just behind the ships.

John Johnson worked for the Tyne Improvement Commission and the Port of Tyne Authority from 1947 until 1992. He is still associated with the river, giving talks about his experiences of working on the Tyne and has provided an informative commentary on its historical background to passengers on river tours:

'I well remember the old foyboatmen on the Tyne. There job was to moor vessels. They worked around the clock as the Tyne waits for no one. Sometimes, when they were going up river, they used to tie their boats to a tug by a rope and on occasions I've seen them being towed upstream at such a speed they were almost at forty-five degrees to the water.

In the past, most goods going to and from Tyne Dock went by railway and there were miles and miles of railway track often with very ramshackle and rotting old railway wagons laying about. Some of the companies, who had premises at the dock, imported pit props and they would be arranged around their yards in huge stacks or loaded into wagons. Then, over the years, as the mines started using hydraulic props, the demand for wooden ones got less and less and the stacks and wagons gradually disappeared. For a while we were left with these vast empty areas. There have been many debates over what to do with redundant areas. The Slake had been filled in before they were sure what they were going to do with it. I think at one time there was a proposal to turn it into a golf course! Eventually other activities moved in, such as the Tyne Car Terminal which serves the Nissan factory at Sunderland. Big ships called 'mother ships' come over from Japan calling at Tyne Dock. They can hold up to nine thousand cars at a time There are also smaller 'feeder ships' which handle around a thousand cars and take them over to Europe. A lot of the cars Nissan sends down to Tyne Dock now leave by rail, loaded on to special wagons and sent via the Channel Tunnel to Italy.

After many years of dwindling away, more freight is beginning to use the dock by rail. The dock handles a lot of aluminium. It comes across from Russia. The Russians pay for many of their imports with aluminium. It belongs to the banks and they have got several warehouses at Tyne Dock stacked from floor to ceiling with aluminium. It's stored in something like a bonded warehouse system and it's handled like it's money, which to them I suppose it is. The old Tyne Dock water area has gradually been filled in, there are offices there now. Part of the site is used as a scrapyard, the towering piles of rusty metal can be seen from the main road and there are new buildings going up.

I am now a National Trust speaker and guide at Souter Lighthouse – the first lighthouse in the world to be powered by electricity. Just off Souter Lighthouse there is a little pillar sticking out of the water. It's obviously man-made and often when I have been up there pointing out details of the coastal area I can see people looking at it, trying to work out what it is and what it was for. I have heard some great theories. One man was convinced it was some kind of early lighthouse, but it was actually put there during the Second World War as a range marker for the Gun Battery at Tynemouth. There would probably have been some kind of flag on top.'

A view of Tyne Dock Pool showing ships loading at the coal staithes. A group of warehouses are to the left. Much of the area here has now been filled in and developed. Indeed the Port of Tyne Authority's own headquarters are probably located about where the ship is at the right of the picture.

Tyne Dock Staithes.

A Monarch postcard view of the Coaling Staithes.

The remains of the staithes, *circa* 1972. The iron ore terminal which supplied the former steelworks at Consett can be seen just behind the front of the ship.

A row of hydraulic travelling cranes at Tyne Dock. They were apparently built by Cowans and Sheldon of Carlisle.

A group of workers in a Tyne Dock timber yard.

Right: An accident involving one of the lever arm grabbing cranes at the dock. We are not sure of the circumstances but it appears the crane is being 'shored up' after the accident.

Tyne Dock Post Office, *circa* 1910. As well as catering to locals it would surely handle a great deal of traffic generated from the river. Seafarers often sent postcards home of the area where they had docked and its possible the office contained an assortment that would delight many of today's collectors.

Vaux off sales at No 1 Napier Street, Tyne Dock. The name above the shop doorway appears to be Elsie Dixon.

Corporation cars 31 and 16 at Tyne Dock. Although they are travelling in opposite directions both cars are bound for the Pier Head. The double wires, positive and negative, required by trolleybuses appear to be in place and this is possibly the last day of tramcar service on 10th April 1938.

Trolleybus No 200 standing in roughly the same location as No 31 in late 1959.

Two views of river postman Bob Plum at work. He used a small row boat to deliver mail to ships moored along the riverbank in South Shields. We believe mail would often arrive before the ship it was intended for docked in the Tyne and there would often be changing of moorings as ships were moved around the Tyne to discharge cargo, undergo repair and pick up new cargo. This would cause some complication to sorting letters for his round. In 1934 Bob retired and we are informed his successor faced added difficulties due to wartime restrictions over information on ship movements.

FRIENDS AND FAMILY

Thomas Dodds Johns with his mother in the back garden of their bungalow in the mid 1960s. Thomas, born in 1907 and one of eleven children, had a long successful showbusiness career starting off at the Alexandra Theatre. At fifteen he left Shields for London to appear in many of the capital's musicals and also travel the country in many touring shows.

What may very well be a children's 'Victory Tea' celebration in 1919. The location is believed to be in the High Shields area. It would be interesting to know how the meal was organised, there would seem to be far too many children to be served at once. Phyllis Stares, aged three, is the girl in the bottom right corner.

Fund raising dogs for the Alexandra Rose Day, 1934. The cart, being pulled by the dogs, was probably made with the wheels from an old perambulator. It carried a box of pale pink artificial roses which purchasers then pinned to their coats.

A street party in Lytton Street in the 1930s. The street is decorated with home-made trellises constructed out of wood and crepe paper roses. The residents have also furnished the street with clippy mats and tables holding indoor plants, creating a slightly surreal effect. The Aspidistra was a favourite household plant as it would grow well in the gloomiest of rooms. Bottom left are the Bruce family: mother, Ganny Clement, Mary Ann, Lottie and Frank Bruce. Just visible is Mrs Rasher on her knees. She had been washing her front step and did not feel tidy or presentable enough to have her photo taken. Towards the right are the Poole family. For occasions such as this the older women would put on a clean pinny and tidy their hair and feel presentable but younger girls, one of whom can be seen mid right, clearly desired a more fashionable image.

Phyllis Thornborrow who lived in Lytton Street recalls:

'A bookie lived at the bottom of our street and we would see people furtively slying into his house to place their bets and you could often hear his name being mentioned in hushed tones. Every now and then we would hear someone dashing into our house which was further up the street. He would be hiding from the police who would periodically raid his home as such betting was illegal in those days.'

Joyce Carlson recalls South Shields had a carnival every year where people would collect for charity:

'They would hire fancy dress costumes and I remember going with my mother to a warehouse to choose one for myself. I always favoured colourful gypsy outfits with gold coins hanging from the headgear. Molly, our Airedale, would wear a Union Jack and with two collection boxes on her back did very well as we paraded through the town. The parades usually ended on 'Clarkies Field' near Eldon Street where there was a fairground. A man who had a flea circus came to the field every year and had a set up with a thread as a tight rope. There was an umbrella attached to a flea who would walk over it. One even rode a three wheeler bike. While this went on some of the other fleas would be feeding on the man's arm and then he would put them back in a little jar while the others finished their act. I think he had about twenty fleas in all.'

Children of Barnes Road School, 1915

A football team from the Prince Albert Charity football match of 1925. The only player known is Joe Carneman.

Lady pensioners of the Wesleyan
chapel, Frederick Street in the
mid 1930s. To the right is Mrs
Urran. The chapel's foundation
stone was laid on 7th June 1881
by Mr J.C. Stevenson. Hodgson
notes that: 'The chapel is in the
classic style of architecture, of
the Queen Anne type, having
two schoolrooms and three
classrooms beneath, with
vestries at the rear. A gallery,
supported by ornamental pillars,
extends round three sides of the
building, with an orchestra
behind the pulpit platform, but
divided from the chapel by a
moulded arch of pillars. The
interior woodwork is of pitched
pine varnished, and the total
cost including the site was
£4,292.'

Mrs Polly, left, and Charlotte
Bruce who attended St Francis'
Church.

Members of the Harniman family in
Bythorne Street: Mr & Mrs George
Harniman with their children George,
Isabel, Annie, Louise Mary and Joe.

The Linn brothers who lived in the
Chichester area.

Mary and Charles Mills, relatives of
the Harniman's, who emigrated to
America.

Miss Elliot, niece of Isabelle
Harniman, *circa* 1900.

The wedding of Sammy Bruce and Joan Prior, *circa* 1945. They are outside St Francis Church, Garwood Street. Sheila Tweddell is on the right.

Memories of the Bents Cottages

Emma Gilpin, who now lives off Emery Street, spent much of her childhood living at the Bents Cottages near the site of Westoe Colliery. She recalls part of her childhood in the area:

'We lived at number 14, my mam's mam lived at number 10 and my father's mam lived at number 23. The Scotts lived at number 8. It was like a great big family. The cottages had huge living rooms with great stone floors – you could get a double bed in the corner of the living room if you had to. Sometimes they used to have sing songs in my nana's house and someone would accompany them on a portable organ. There was a lot of sharing and borrowing going on, particularly if meals had to be made. Often a bowl of rice pudding or something would be sent down the street for a neighbour's children if someone had made too much of it on a Sunday. The old men were never left alone. My mother would tell me, "Go and see Granddad Powel," or "Go and see if Granddad Tindal is alright." We would sometimes play card games with them for a while. This was how I learned to play patience. All my mam's brothers married people from the Bents except Les who married someone from Stanhope Road. That was almost like bringing a stranger into the family. When I look back I think they all just married neighbours. Two doors up from the Scotts was a Mr Thompson. For some reason people used to call him Swallow. He had one arm and used to work in the signal box behind Tadema Road that controlled the line for the Marsden Rattler up to Whitburn. We used to die to get up into the box. Sometimes Mrs Thompson sent us up there with his dinner and he used to let us pull the lever for the points when the Rattler was due to pass by. Walter Main had a little shop in Lord Street. It was really old fashioned shop even then. There was someone there who would buy our sweet coupons off us and we would use the money to buy sweets with what coupons we had left.'

Members of the Home Guard. The location appears to be Westoe Cricket Ground.

The Home Guard Rocket Battery in Northfield Gardens, 1945-6. Frederick Boad is in t[

rom the front, 11th from right. William Bohill is in the 2nd front row, 4th from left.

A family group – Mary, Tom, Hilda Victoria and Beatrice Best, 1933.

Tom Best recalls: 'There were eight of us in the family. Dad went to sea with the Merchant Navy and often it was one and two year trips in those days while Mam looked after us full time. She made most of the girls' dresses as well as all our meals. In the mornings I would go to the outside washhouse to put the boiler on for my mother. With six children she was washing almost all day, everyday, but when we came home from school at mid-day she would always have a dinner ready for us. In the early 1930s my sisters had to go into domestic service in the South of England because they could not find work up here. My father's ship, the *Avondale Park*, was the last merchant vessel to be torpedoed in Europe during the Second World War. It happened the day before VE Day. A U-boat, U2336, under the command of Korvettenkapitan Emil Klusmeyer had set sail from Christiansand on 1st May 1945. Klusmeyer had been involved in the development of tactics to be used by U-boats similar to U2336. He apparently failed to receive a signal transmitted on 4th May ordering all boats to cease hostilities and return to base. He attacked a convoy off May Island in the entrance to the Firth of Forth at 00.40 on 8th May sinking the Norwegian freighter *Sneland* and the *Avondale Park* with a spread of two torpedoes. Two of Dad's fellow crewmen were killed and he arrived home on VE Day all bandaged up. He had been torpedoed twice before that. When he was at sea he sent home only £2 10s a month and my mother had to be helped out by the Assistance Board which was known as the Guardians. We had also received Guardian money during the 1926 Strike and I think all of that money had to be paid back. My dad retired when he was 65 and died at the age of 68.'

Children of Mortimer Road Infants School, 1933. Included is Joyce Hindmarch now Joyce Grant.

Children of Mortimer Road Juniors School, 1950.

Pupils of Mortimer Road School, 1954.

The Mortimer Road School netball team at a practice session in the senior schoolyard in 1955. Included are: Maureen Coull, Ann Moore, Pat Eden, Pamela Drummond, Linda Boag and Margaret Stewart

Mortimer Road School pupils playing 'Rounders' on the playing fields behind the school, 1955.

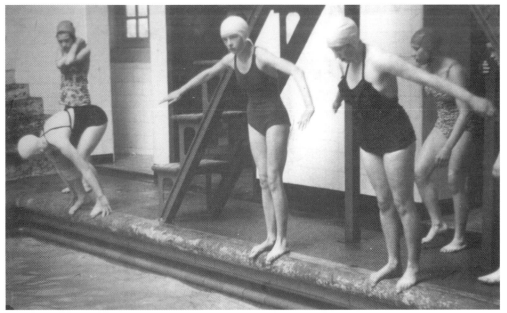

Pupils of Mortimer Road Senior School during their annual swimming gala held at Derby Street baths, 1954. Included are Margaret Stewart, Maureen Lamb and Anita Hunt.

Mortimer Road School sports day at Cleadon Park in 1954. Included are: Ann Stephenson, Margaret Stewart and Anita Hunt.

Mr Atkinson's class of second year seniors at Mortimer Road School in 1955.

Above: Eva Harniman, stage name Eva Sheldon. At the age of four she started her stage career with the Thorburns who ran the Alexandra Players at the Alexandra Theatre in Wallace Street. She went on to become a leading light at the London Palladium and starred in *Cinderella* with Jack Bucannan as Buttons. She also acted with the Crazy Gang.

Above right: Irene Bennett (now Foster), 1957. She has been a staunch member of Harton Methodist Church throughout her life. She also worked in Lock's Newsagency in Prince Edward Road.

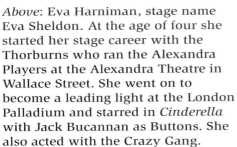

Right: Gladys Hunter. Along with her sister she ran a post office in Mortimer Road. She was a long term friend of actor, dancer and singer Thomas Dodds Johns.

Children of Trinity School around the maypole in the late 1930s. Included is Ella Reay. The school was built in 1836 on land given by the Dean and Chapter of Durham at a cost of £516 13s and 8d. Closed during the evacuation, the boys' school was destroyed by bombing in 1941. Pupil numbers gradually dwindled as pre and post-war slum clearance drives gradually moved families out of its catchment area. In later years many of the classes were of mixed age giving it a family feel. It finally shut its doors in 1971. The building was later used by Selby's Garage.

Lady Chapman presenting gifts sent across from America to local nursing cadets. The date is 1941 and the location near the Town Hall in Broughton Road. Also present are: Dr Lyons, Olive Hope and Annie Madison.

Children at South Shields Greyhound Stadium watch a magic trick performed by Tommy Duffy. Tommy went on to become a popular local and international entertainer under the name of Alan Fox.

A party held at No 46 Morpeth Avenue to celebrate the birthday of Marti Young (holding her birthday present). She is with a group of her friends who lived nearby.

Members of the Tweddell and Thornborrow families at Christmas. Included are: Stan, Sheila, Neil & Sandra Tweddell and Phyllis & Richard Thornborrow.

Richard Thornborrow, September 1941. He began work with the South Shields, Jarrow and Hebburn Co-operative Society as an errand boy and went on to become grocery manager. He was with the society for 41 years. During the Second World War he served in the Eighth Army as a store corporal in Egypt and Sicily.

A publicity photograph of local band Hearts in Amour taken on the Town Hall staircase in the mid 1980s.

Members of the Cleadon Club on an outing, *circa* 1962.

Samuel Bruce, Tugboat Master. Seafaring ran in the Bruce family – when his brother, Albert John Bruce, passed away in April 1911 his obituary was featured in the local press:

'Few shipmasters in the Tyne district were able to show such a good record of brave deeds performed at sea as captain Albert John Bruce, whose remains were placed in their last resting place on Saturday afternoon in Smithdown Road Cemetery, Liverpool. He passed away in the early hours of last Thursday morning after an illness of ten days. Captain Bruce was a son of the late John Bailey Bruce who was for many years ballast inspector in the employ of the Tyne Improvement Commissioners. During his sea career the late Captain Bruce had been responsible for saving large numbers of his fellow creatures from certain death under the most pernicious of circumstances and Captain Bruce had an honoured place among the brave men of the British Mercantile Marine. Among the testimonials he was presented with was a handsome silver cup from the British Government and the Mercantile Marine Service Association's illuminated vote of thanks for his rescue of the crew of the British barqueritine *Chislehurst* on 27th February 1893 in the North Atlantic during a hurricane. Three years later, while in command of the North Shields SS *Stag*, he was instrumental in saving the crew of the American schooner *Ennity R. Dyer*, who were rescued from their sinking vessel after drifting about the Atlantic Ocean for 12 days. The American Government later awarded Captain Bruce a valuable gold watch and chain suitably inscribed. Captain Bruce's last command was that of the SS *Harlow*, which sailed from the Tyne in the May of last year and proceeded to Newport News where she took on board American troops for conveyance to the Philippine Islands. The deceased was one of the best known and highly respected shipmasters of Tyneside.'

Flo Thorburn in costume for the role of Cinderella at the Alexandra Theatre in Wallace Street, *circa* 1930s.

Joyce Carlson recalls:

'I have quite a lot of memories of early childhood and No 20 Alma Street where I was born. My parents were obsessed with the theatre and always took me along with them. Some of the images which have influenced me immensely in my paintings I saw with them at various performances. One evening, when I was about two, I can remember seeing a beautiful blond lady in a pale yellow dress on stage. The limelight bathed her in a golden hue and I remember the dress had a lot of frills. I was so taken up with it my mother bought me a frilly dress of the same colour. In 1998 I bumped into Joan Mullen a friend of mine and we talked about our early childhood and she said she had some old photographs of her parents who worked at the Alexandra Theatre for 10 years. She brought the photos to my house and as you may have guessed two of them were of her mother dressed in the same outfit from all those years ago. The show had been Cinderella. The image was slightly different because of cause it was in black and white and there was none of the footlights and limelight. But there was no mistake that this was the person I had been so impressed with all those years ago. Limelight is so called because theatre spotlights were originally oil powered with lime added to the oil to increase the brilliance of the light.'

May Anderson and Muriel Gardner (now Hanson) outside Muriel's house in Commercial Road in 1951. May lived in Glasgow and her husband was a friend of Muriel's husband. In their youth, May travelled to South Shields and met Muriel through their husband's. They stayed in contact by letter and in 1999 May travelled from Glasgow to Shields to stay for a week with Muriel. This was their first meeting for thirty years. They are pictured below outside Muriel's house in Ullswater Gardens.

SECTION THREE

TRAVEL AND TOURISM

Thomas Lenny and his sister Audrey riding a stuffed zebra on South Shields promenade in 1947.

The old railway station near the market place. This served as the town's main passenger station from 1842 to 1879 when it closed in favour of a new terminus in Mile End Road. At one point an overall roof seems to have covered the platform and tracks. In 1855 the station was the subject of a letter of complaint to the editor of the *Shields Gazette* from one Fred Barclay:

Sir.-

Allow me through your columns to call attention to a local evil of public importance. I allude to the inconvenient manner in which the tickets are issued at the South Shields Railway Station. Perhaps the evil cannot be caused to appear in a stronger light than by a comparison with the mode adopted at North Shields where a policeman prevents crowding and all is orderly and businesslike. At South Shields the public are obliged to congregate in the dirty little room in which the tickets are issued until the train is at the platform, and the station clerk chooses to raise the slide, when a rush occurs, and a state of indescribable confusion commences, in which bonnets are crushed, dresses are torn, toes tread upon, and a fine opportunity afforded to the pickpocket to exercise his calling. Yet by opening the office ten minutes sooner all of which I complain would be avoided; and although it might occasion a little chill in this cold weather to the clerk that sits upon the stool within, it will confer a great benefit upon the public.'

The rather 'happy go lucky' style of early railway management seems to have killed five passengers at the station in 1844. Hodson notes that at that time although the line from South Shields to Brockley Whins was double tracked, trains actually ran each way on both with one track reserved for coal traffic and the other passengers. At 5 am on 8th October 1844 a special one coach train for the conveyance of butchers to the Newcastle cattle markets left Shields drawn 'tender first' by the locomotive, 'Nelson'. After a short while the driver observed another engine, the 'Leopard', heading towards them on the same track. Both crews put their locomotives into reverse and jumped from their cabs. In the collision the Nelson's tender was derailed, but the locomotive remained on the track. Crewless and with its motion reversed it began pushing the carriage back towards Shields, reaching what then must have been the terrifying speed of 50 mph before it dashed into the station and smashed the carriages of the 5.45 mail train. Five passengers were killed.

In 1940 Joyce Carlson's parents' lodger, Arthur Appleby, worked for the Co-operative Wholesale Society at Boldon Lane. Joyce only had to attend school five half days a week due to shelter construction work at her school. On Monday afternoons he would pick up the notes for the weekly grocery order, to be delivered the following Friday. Aged eleven she recalls visiting the old station, then in use as a house, with him to take their order: 'A family lived there with seven sons. When we called the mother would put the kettle on straight away and make a fuss of me and say she always wanted a daughter like me. Needless to say I thought she was a lovely woman and looked forward to going to her house every second Monday.'

An advertisement for the Royal Hotel on the corner of Mile End Road and Ocean Road. At first glance this building can be difficult to place. The hotel's facilities included a grand coffee room, ladies drawing room, commodious commercial room, reading, arbitration, auction and assembly rooms, stock rooms, private sitting rooms, billiard, smoking and club rooms, en suit bath rooms and lavatories and extensive dining rooms.

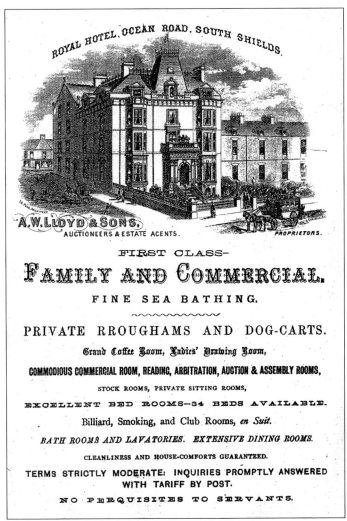

The Wheatsheaf Hotel, *circa* 1925. Around this time hotels such as this were being advertised as watering holes rather than as places to stay. Possibly visitors were graduating to the long line of boarding houses in Ocean Road.

A town guide of 1928 enthused: 'The thriving town of South Shields, which has in recent years by reason of the development of its natural advantages, become a recognised seaside resort, is situated on the south bank of the Tyne opposite the somewhat better known watering place of Tynemouth. It is situated to be precise in lat 55.0 N, long 1.26 E. It is around 270 miles or six and a half hours journey by rail from London (Kings Cross). South Shields is served by the North Eastern Railway running in connection with the Great Northern from London, the Midland from the Midlands and the North British from Scotland. By sea the journey from London to the Tyne is made in about twenty hours in well appointed steamers, furnished with all the modern appliances for comfortable transit and lit by electric light. The steamers sail from Free Wharf, Ratclife (London) on Wednesdays and Saturdays There is also a passenger service from Aberdeen, Dundee and Leith.'

Right: An advertisement from a visitors' guide. It is curious to realise that even in the mid 1920s the fact that most of the town was wired for electricity was still seen as something worth promoting in a holiday guide.

VISITORS
TO
SOUTH SHIELDS

will find all Hotels and many Private Residential Apartments fitted with

ELECTRIC LIGHT

affording facilities for the use of electric irons and other useful apparatus.

Voltage 110 *or* 220 *Volts according to location.*

An advertisement for the Golden Lion
Hotel, King Street, *circa* 1920.

Below: Mayor Samuel Lawlan, who will
return later in this book, in the Golden
Lion's entrance. The hotel seems to
have been a favourite place for the
town's dignitaries and businessmen to
entertain visiting dignitaries and
businessmen. It was here that members
of the Corporation entertained Major-
General Hutchinson on 10th November
1882 after his inspection of the horse
tram lines they had just constructed, no
doubt hoping that he would approve
them, even though they had been
constructed to a narrower gauge than
specified by Parliament. To the
Corporation's vast embarrassment he
didn't, and they had to seek new
powers.

A series of images of the Savoy Cinema, Ocean Road, taken in 1936, presumably during the opening week. Seating capacity was just over 1,000 and the screen was reputed to be the biggest in the North East of England. The car park was the site of the Grand Electric Theatre. The reopening of the Savoy hit a snag when the Council apparently refused an entertainment license on the eve of the first performance, 'Goldilocks and the Three Bears', even though the Mayor was already due to attend. When the Savoy was demolished in 1987 there were plans to build old people's flats on the site and later a Quick Fit exhaust centre. Perhaps to the surprise of very few the empty site remains as an eyesore to this day. Looking at images of the building now its difficult to see how the town could have allowed its demolition or could ever be capable of paying for the construction of something like it again.

57

OCEAN ROAD. SOUTH SHIELDS.

10721.J

An unusual postcard view of the middle of Ocean Road, looking towards the Pier Head.

Ocean Road in 1982. Reputedly Ocean Road had at that time the largest number of curry houses for its length in the North East.

The Sea Hotel. When it opened to the public in 1936 the Corporation would still be actively clearing slums and the building's design would surely have aroused all kind of comments from 'very stylish' to 'carbuncle'. It's easy to imagine in pre-war days a couple of the more well-off visitors motoring into the town along the Coast Road, heads turning along the promenade as they passed Gandhi's Temple then their car swinging into the hotel's car park. The Sea Hotel can almost be described as one of Shields' 'forgotten' buildings. Apparently some time after the Second World War, management lost the hotel's records and in 1986 staff only found out about the building's impending fiftieth anniversary when the first manager, Mr Charles Robinson, walked into the lobby and asked if they were doing anything to celebrate the event. Although its not unlikely that some famous names stayed there in the 1930s, or at least stopped in at the bar for a drink, we haven't been able to find out who. However, more recently Leo Sayer and the Nolan Sisters have stayed there, and one of the more recent owners was called Fred Basset. The area around the hotel has at least one claim to fame – it saw one of the town's earliest recorded balloon landings. In August 1887, one launched from the Newcastle Exhibition Park came down in the vacinity. A Hebburn miner, Richard Cole, was the first of thousands soon on the scene, and seeing the balloon's grapple iron dragging across the first rail of the Tyne Improvement Commissions railway he secured it to the second.

The changing face of the North Beach. The above image, dated 1924, is typical of many postcards of the time. *Below*: The same location, *circa* 1984. Powerboats, wetsuits and skis have replaced the sailboats and semi-formal attire of the previous picture.

Members of 274th Field Regiment, Royal Artillery Territorial Army, with a flower display in the North Marine Park in 1960. A photograph of the display was used on the regimental Christmas cards.

The rock archway in the North Marine Park.

Right: An advertisement for Mitchelson's Motor Boat Trips.

Around 1925 a town guide was proclaiming that: 'Rowing boats may be hired by the half hour or hour from boatmen at the North Beach and the South Pier affording interesting excursions and exercise to good oarsmen. Boating is popular at South Shields, and on a fine summer's evening the calm water in the spacious harbour is dotted here and there with happy rowing parties. Fishing is also indulged in from these boats, good hauls of whiting, codling mackerel and other varieties in season being obtainable from the harbour, and outside in finer weather, to the south of the South Pier. Lines and bait can also be obtained on application to boatmen on the beach and at the South Pier. During the summer season large motor boats, licensed by the Board of Trade to accommodate up to 71 passengers, in charge of experienced boatmen, run trips within the harbour, from the North Beach, as well as up river to Ryton; northward to St Mary's Island; and southward to Marsden Rock (keeping within three miles of the shore). Passengers embark at the North Beach, and the large number who do so is evidence of the popularity of these trips.'

MOTOR BOAT TRIPS
—RIVER and SEA—

River Trips to RYTON WILLOWS—2 hours each way.
Sea Trips to ST. MARY'S ISLANDS, MARSDEN ROCK and ROUND THE HARBOUR
Fishing Excursions. — Evening Cruises.
—— Parties of 30 to 260 persons. ——
(Large Parties can be arranged for).
Motor Boats Licensed by Board of Trade.

THE OLD FIRM
MITCHELSON
Landing Stages on North and South Beaches.
Secretaries of Clubs, Works, etc. invited to apply for terms and dates.
Address -
55 St. Aidan's Terrace, SOUTH SHIELDS

Right: Richard Fox at the open air swimming pool on the North Foreshore. Richard was born in Corstorphine Town in 1897 and was a fireman with the South Shields Fire Brigade.

A group in front of the *Tyne* Lifeboat. In days gone by this craft was apparently something of a tourist attraction. In 1887 it was displayed at the Royal Exhibition in Newcastle. The guide commented:

'The famous lifeboat the *Tyne* is at present the only craft on the lake situated in the North Gardens. The *Tyne*, which has been the means of saving 1,024 lives, was the second lifeboat built for service at the river entrance. The first one, which is only known as "The Original" commenced her career in 1790, and while endeavouring to rescue a crew in 1830 was driven on to the rocks and split in two. It was to succeed this vessel that the *Tyne* was presented to the port by Mr Thomas Forrest, a South Shields shipowner, her builders being Messrs John Oliver and Sons, whose premises were at the Lawe, on land afterwards used by Messrs J. Readhead and Co for iron shipbuilding. The exact time when she was constructed is not known, but it is believed to be fifty-five or fifty-six years ago. The last service rendered by the *Tyne* was in 1882. On the 5th December in that year the Norwegian brig *Olaf Kyrre* got upon the Herd Sands. The *Tyne* took the men off her, and a day or two later she saved two men from a schooner named the *Flidat* the same place. The vessel now being exhibited is the property of the Tyne Lifeboat Trust Fund, of which Mr George Lyall is the secretary and Mr Andrew Harrison the lifeboat superintendent. The latter who has occupied his present position for about fourteen years, has been a coxswain since 1858, and a lifeboatman altogether 51 years.'

The North Beach looking towards the Pier Head blockyard. The young boy is Peter Headly.

Below: The Pier Head in winter, with Frankie's Cafe. There are some interesting contrasts in this image. The snow and sea battling for possession of the rocky beach, the boarded up cafes and the burnt out car.

A postcard view of the promenade.

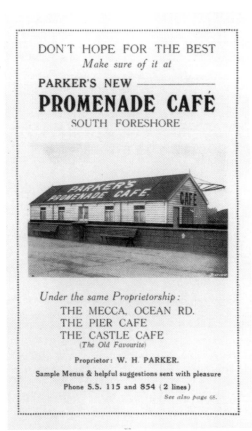

An advertisement for Parker's Cafe.

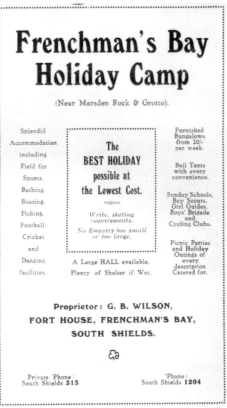

An advertisement for a Holiday Camp at Frenchman's Bay. This may have utilised buildings from the former army camp, but the authors would welcome further information.

The famous St Hilda Professional Band with musical director Lieutenant
Horace Grey CBA, performing in South Marine Park bandstand on Good Friday,
19th April 1935. This was the opening engagement of their annual nationwide
summer tour. As the only ever professional brass band in this country it
enjoyed great success during its ten year career until disbandment in 1937. It
previously existed as the world's renowned and legendary St Hilda Colliery
Band – London Crystal Palace winners of the 1,000 Guineas Challenge Trophy
in 1912, 1920, 1921, 1924 and 1926.

An advertisement for the Economic bus service, *circa* 1928. A contemporary town guide described the company's operation: 'A fifteen minutes bus service is run by Messrs Anderson & Wilson from the terminus in Ocean Road (opposite Council School) to the village of Whitburn, with stopping stages at the Town Hall, Westoe, Harton, Marsden (for Marsden Rock) to Sea Lane, Whitburn. The fares are reasonable and the service is increasing in public favour. The buses are well appointed and run to a specified timetable.'

Below: An Economic at Whitburn heading into South Shields. Although the original company is no more, the name was later revived by South Shields Busways and the distinction between it and the former Corporation services even survived the Stagecoach buy-out, although it now seems to be fading.

An advertisement extolling the virtues of South Shields Corporation Transport, *circa* 1928. The car pictured, 'Nelson', is one of a number of the Corporation's own rebuilds from around 1926. A tramway journal described how the lower deck of an identical rebuild, No 14, was finished off in specially selected figured oak, the roof lining being of maple. The new top cover was constructed out of pitch pine framing, the side boards being of five ply Mahogany. The interior was finished of in a Cuban Mahogany and pitch pine. The Corporation seems to have begun supplementing its tram services with bus routes shortly before the

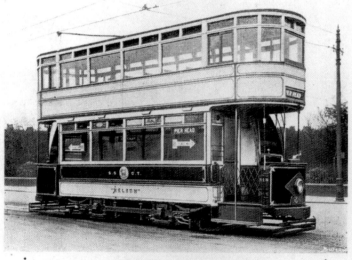

S.S.C.T.

"THE BEST WAY."

This is YOUR Car — Use it!

"NELSON."

Pre-War Fares.   Pullman Comfort.

1¼ miles for a Penny.
2d. ALL THE WAY.

Comfortable and Hand-polished Transverse Seats, Electric Heaters, full size Bevelled Mirrors, and ———— Civility.

SPEED.   COMFORT.   SAFETY.

Telephone - South Shields 157.

First World War. The earliest the authors know of was the battery electric bus service between Stanhope Road and Simonside via Green Lane which began operating in July 1914. These buses may also have been the Corporation's first petrol buses as they were converted from electric operation shortly after the First World War.

A late 1920s South Shields Corporation Transport advertisement featuring a thirty seater Guy omnibus purchased around 1928 for the Cleadon Estate to High Shields Station via Mortimer Road service. In the early 1920s the number of Corporation and private motor buses in the town began increasing. Although the battery buses had been a financial success, the Corporation's pre-war motor bus services seem to have often run at an overall loss and it is possible their provision was motivated more by protectionism against private operators, such as the Northern General Transport Company, as much as to provide a public service. Around 1926 it was remarked that while the Corporation

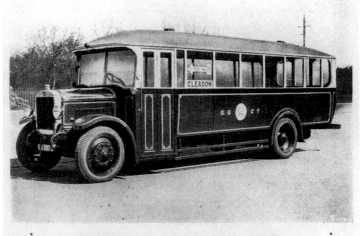

S.S.C.T.

"THE BEST WAY."

Be sure it is a Corporation Bus and ——————— Ride in Comfort.

EASY. :: LOW LOAD LINE.
UPHOLSTERED SPRING SEATS.

FAST, COMFORTABLE AND SAFE.

Wait for the Crimson Lake and Cream Bus.

Ask for the Bus with a Name.

Telephone - South Shields 157.

II

seemed keen for its own buses to 'go a roving' for trade beyond the Borough boundaries it also wanted to ring fence private operators out of the town in an almost medieval fashion which included restrictions on private operators setting down and picking up passengers in the borough.

A line up of Northern buses, apparently dating from the mid 1920s at the official opening of the Northern depot in South Shields in 1929.

A Northern bus, possibly one used on a Newcastle-bound service, outside the depot in Mile End Road.

A Corporation trolleybus climbs the bank from the Coast Road up towards the Marsden Inn. Visible behind it is the former Marsden Rattler railway bridge. One of the authors recalls walking down this bank carrying a bucket and spade after getting off an Economic bus. The bridge had marvellous acoustics that made it possible to produce a very annoying (to grown ups) echo if you screeched loud enough. When the day at the beach was over and the time for the steep climb back up the bank to the bus stop came around, metal spades would be dragged along the tarmac walkway no doubt further aggravating the migraine that many adults seemed to be suffering at this point.

National Coal Board 0-6-0 Hunslet diesel locomotive 506 returning from Westoe to Whitburn Colliery on 11th April 1968. The colliery closed three months later. This view was probably taken from the footbridge that crossed the line at Marsden Grotto.

A postcard view of Marsden Grotto.

The possibilities of earning money through tourism at Marsden Bay first seems to have been realised by a miner at Marsden Quarry nicknamed 'Jack the Blaster'. Originally an Allenhead miner, Jack and his wife took up residence in one of the caves towards the centre of the bay around 1782. As they became older and the number of visitors to the bay increased, some doubtless being drawn by the couples unusual residence, their income was increasingly supplemented by selling refreshments to tourists. In 1815 Jack apparently cut a set of steps down to the bay which became known as 'Jack the Blaster's stairs'.

In 1828 the couple were succeeded by Peter Allen a former gamekeeper then working at the Marsden Quarries who began to enlarge their cave and used the rock debris to form a quay in front of the cliff. At first he lived in the cave only in the summer, moving to Whitburn the remainder of the year. Later he became a permanent resident selling refreshments to visitors. He constructed a series of steps up Marsden Rock allowing visitors to reach its summit. He also drove a shaft through the roof of one of the caves at the Grotto facilitating the provisioning of his residence.

However, Allen had apparently just set up shop without formally acquiring the land. In 1848 the lessees of the adjoining lands, which included Andrew Stoddart, the Dean and Chapter of Durham's agents and John Clay, who a short time later became the first Mayor of South Shields, made a claim on Allen for rent. Allen claimed he had made the Grotto on his own and owed suit and service to no man. The case was tried at the Durham Assizes in early 1850. We believe public sympathy was largely with Peter Allen on the matter and there was a feeling that he had been 'duped' by John Clay and the others, being allowed to build and make a success of the Grotto before they pressed claim for ownership. Apparently around that time there was a popular public notion that owners of land would 'appear and disappear' as it suited them. If land contained former cess pits, industrial waste or was otherwise a danger to the public then those responsible for it would hide behind a tangle of age old leases and rights. However, should any person or body clear the hazard in the public interest, the owners would miraculously appear as if from thin air and quickly build slum houses or otherwise make use of the land for their own profit. Judgement largely went against Allen, although a compromise was arrived at where he agreed to take a lease of the Grotto for 21 years. This seems to have involved a £50 payment that was either back rent or a fine from the excise department and an additional £10 each year in rent. Allen died that same year. Shortly afterwards the following account of a visit to the Grotto was written:

'From the sweet little village of Westoe, we took an easterly course, by the sea banks; and at length, after passing a white farm-house and crossing a tiny bridge, we arrived at the zigzag flight of steps that led to the Grotto. Descending these somewhat steep stairs, we landed a few yards from the entrance to Peter Allen's door. A couple of dogs ran up to us, saluting us with a bark; but instinctively knowing we were friends to the house, did not bite. Mrs Allen, who had been appraised by her sentinels of our arrival, came forwards to meet us, and assured us into the front bar, where we partook of some slight refreshment, and commenced chatting with her on ordinary topics. A fresh, fair-looking young man attracted our attention, as he bore a striking resemblance to his father, especially in the expression of the eyes; for there were the laughter-loving devils in their corners, so peculiar to the "old man". A dark-eyed maiden now made her appearance, dressed with great simplicity, wearing a Holland jacket that fitted tightly and displayed the graceful symmetry of her form. Her face is interesting, unassuming and yet indicative of considerable mental activity; and we were told that her courage is of the "Darling" school, and, without the slightest fear, she can heave on the stormy wave. She is also an admirable shot, and can provide a sparrow pie for her friends on the shortest notice.

THE BALL-ROOM, MARSDEN GROTTO.

The interior of the Ball Room.

But where was Peter all this time? Alas! "The widow's sombre cap" reveals the melancholy absence. Death has been at Marsden Rock; the grim desolator has quenched the light and soul of that social hermitage for ever! Peter Allen the bold, intrepid, the free hearted-is sleeping in his silent grave; and the sea waves still nestle round his much loved rock, murmuring his requiem. When he saw the home he had hollowed out of the stony cliff in which he had toiled and hoped for many a circling year, and the inheritance of his offspring, might be torn from them – when he marked his enemies secretly undermining his dearest anticipations – the blow was too much for him: he refused to be comforted, and calmly laid himself down to die. Peace to his memory!'

The account also detailed a tour of the Grotto:

'In a room upstairs are several cases of stuffed animals and birds among which we discovered two finely plumed ravens. One was a great favourite of Peter's.

The construction of the lift shaft at Marsden Grotto, 1937.

He lost a leg by an unlucky shot of a sportsman who did not know to whom he belonged. Poor "Ralph" had lived fourteen years in the Grotto, and was accidentally killed by the bite of a greyhound in whose kennel he roosted every night.

We were shown the "Gaol room"; so called from a large grated frame of iron being fixed to the wall as in prison. The "Devil's Chamber", and the circular dining and ball rooms (120 feet long) were shown in succession. At the southern extremity of the ball room is a large excavation which has not received any finishing touches but still retains all its roughage, apparently fresh from the picks of the excavators. It is lighted, in the day time, by a huge aperture equally unfinished; and it affords a cool and fitting retirement for the dancers, or in the shades of evening when left to its pristine gloominess, it may serve as a very secluded spot for some happy pair who have become enamoured of each other during the bewitching motions of a waltz or quadrille; and may thereafter be entitled the "Lover's Retreat".'

Tourists would have been drawn to the area by the beauty of Marsden Bay. It's also likely during the second half of the 19th century many would find the area would provide an excellent vantage point to watch the slow advance of two of the wonders of the age, the north and south piers, into the German Ocean. In 1874 the Grotto was taken over by Sidney Miles Hawkes, a flamboyant man and a great believer in the cause of Italian freedom. Hawkes apparently filled the Grotto with his personality and turned it into a mixture of Cafe Royal, El Vino and the Mabillion. He retired from the Grotto in 1882.

Like George Washington's hammer, which had a series of different heads and shafts but everyone still recognises it as the same old hammer, the buildings at Marsden Grotto have been rebuilt and refurbished many times. In 1989 it was refurbished at a cost of £200,000 while in the year 2000 it was standing boarded up and ransacked after a dispute resulted in its sudden, and we hope temporary, closure. According to the media the building was abandoned so suddenly that thieves, in scenes reminiscent of the movie *Whisky Galore*, looted spirits, fixtures and fittings before the premises could be secured.

Repairs being undertaken to the South Pier in August 1959 after damage caused by *Sir John Snell*. Although the Tyne Improvement Commission crane has long since been cut up for scrap the 'tongs' being used to lower the block survive at the Tanfield Railway, Gateshead. They appear to have been kept in the blockyard at the end of the pier on a dedicated rail wagon, which also survives at the Tanfield Railway, and only brought out when needed.

One of the other surviving items of rolling stock from the Tyne Improvement Commission Railway is a van which seems to have been used to convey personnel along the pier. The body at least seems to have been in use on the pier from around the turn of the century. It is seen here on the John Reid Road being transported to Beamish Open Air Museum where it is now preserved.

A British Railways diesel multiple unit just outside of Westoe Colliery in 1989. This is not a passenger service or enthusiasts' special but a train full of track test equipment. The former Harton Coal Company line was in the process of being upgraded to allow British Rail locomotives to move coal wagons between Westoe and Tyne Dock.

An immaculately turned out Wright's Biscuits' van. Wright's supplied biscuits across much of the UK and we presume beyond. We are sure there will be an interesting story behind the company obtaining the '1234' phone number.

The Flying Scotsman at Tyne Dock Station on 7th September 1968. The visit was part of the East Coast Rail tour. Almost all of the buildings in this view have since been demolished.

A British Railways multiple unit passing construction work on South Shields Metro station. The date is likely to be early 1981 and, at this point in time, single line working operated between this South Shields and Tyne Dock. The rail service was withdrawn in June 1981.

The Harton Coal Company's Victoria Road coal depot, *circa* 1900. South Shields Corporation's Victoria Road depot is to the right. The image is one of an extensive series of photographs detailing the HCC's properties.

A National Coal Board tipping lorry, *circa* 1960. The back of the lorry is partitioned to allow loads for different customers to be efficiently unloaded.

A Pickford's removals vehicle transporting a heavy load under police escort. The convoy appears to be moving from Prince Edward Road to King George Road.

A row of trucks and vans that the authors believe belonged to local haulage contractor Warden Newby. The location is thought to be the Victoria Road area.

SECTION FOUR

A MAYOR'S OWN STORY

The robing of Councillor Samuel Lawlan as Mayor on the morning of 9th November 1933. Others in the group are: Councillor J.B. Potts, Mr George McVay (Mayor's secretary), Alderman G.H. Linney (retiring Mayor), Mr Harold Ayrey (Town Clerk) and Alderman Edward Smith (proposer). His daughter, Margaret, collated a scrapbook of photographs and cuttings covering his time in office. It is from this book, kindly lent by his granddaughter, Mary McNeaney, that this chapter is drawn. His year was probably not the most remarkable in the town's history, but it occurred at a kind of high point in the Council's power and responsibility. It was after the years in which much of the town we know today had been put together from plans and schemes formed by officials in the Town Hall, and quite possibly at unofficial meetings in the back rooms of local pubs, then hammered out in the Council Chamber. Around a decade later post-war thinking would see many of the Council's responsibilities handed over to national organisations.

Samuel Lawlan's first public act as Mayor was the fixing of the first poppy to a wreath that the patrons of the Scala Cinema were to lay on the Westoe War Memorial. On the same day his wife, Mary, (pictured left) who naturally served as Mayoress, was at a gathering of South Shields and District Nursing Association in St Michael's Hall. Here, Lady Readhead presents Mrs Dunlop with the first prize for Whist. Also present are Mrs Readhead, Miss Blakey, Nurse Cook and Mrs Jobson.

Mr Lawlan was first elected to the Council as a Moderate Representative of the Westoe Ward in 1925 and became an Alderman in 1936. His father was Captain Andrew Lawlan whose ship the SS *Tyne* was wrecked on the South Pier in the great storm of 21st December 1876 with the loss of all hands. Apparently, at the age of 14, Samuel heard distress guns firing while sitting by the fireside with his mother. Knowing her husband's ship was due she sent him off to make enquiries. When he reached the beach, wreckage was washing ashore and he was told that it was his father's ship that had gone down taking all hands with it.

Samuel began his working life serving as an apprentice seaman on sailing ships in two of the then well known South Shields barques, the *British Constitution* and the *Northern Light*. He was appointed master of the North Shields boat *Woodhorn* at the age of 25. During the First World War he was attached to the staff of the Principal Naval Transport Officer in France and was stationed at Dieppe where he was mentioned in dispatches. On his retirement he bought the schooner *Annie* which carried coal between Seaham Harbour and the Cromarty Firth. When it came to grief he bought a large amount of house property in Shields. In politics he was described as hard working and plain spoken and having an independence of thought and action in Council and Committee which were often a disturbing factor in his own party ranks.

He was vice chairman of the Public Assistance Committee for some time. When he was unanimously elected Mayor on the 9th October 1933, the local press made full use of nautical metaphors in reporting his accession suggesting that the breezy old salt was a worthy captain of the Shields ship of state, and that he would steer a straight course though a good deal of stormy weather was expected.

In his inaugural speech Mr Lawlan stressed that it was the job of Mayor to rule but not govern. He also said: 'I have a great and sincere sympathy for the poor and I have sympathy for the rich because they have many trial and tribulations which are not appreciated by the looker on.' He also made reference to the Corporation's large role in the running of the town, saying: 'It was true that from the cradle to the grave townspeople were all more or less indebted to the Corporation for their comfort and happiness.'

Mayor's Sunday. Church Parade.

ST. HILDA'S CHURCH.

Mayor - - COUNCILLOR S. LAWLAN.

Order of Procession.

ROYAL NAVAL VOLUNTEER RESERVES—
    LT.-COMMANDER W. CARNALL, M.C., D.S.M., R.N.V.R.
74TH NORTHUMBERLAND BRIGADE, R.F.A.—
    LT.-COL. R. ATKINSON, M.C., T.D., R.A. (T.A.)
1ST DURHAM CADET BATTALION—
    LT.-COL. L. EDWARDS, Commanding.
BRITISH LEGION, SOUTH SHIELDS BRANCH.
VETERANS ASSOCIATION, SOUTH SHIELDS BRANCH.
VOLUNTEER LIFE BRIGADE—CAPT. J. PAGE, M.B.E.
SOUTH SHIELDS PILOTS.
ST. JOHN AMBULANCE BRIGADE—ST. HILDA DIVISION, BOROUGH
    DIVISION AND NURSING DIVISION.
THE BOYS BRIGADE—CAPTAIN JAMES MURRAY.
SEA SCOUTS AND BOY SCOUTS.
SOUTH SHIELDS TRAMWAYMEN.
RIVER TYNE POLICE—CHIEF CONSTABLE D. ATKINSON.
SOUTH SHIELDS BOROUGH POLICE.
ST. HILDA COLLIERY BAND.
THE TOWN CLERK.   THE MAYOR.   THE DEPUTY MAYOR.
ALDERMEN BY SENIORITY.   COUNCILLORS BY SENIORITY.
THE JUSTICES AND THEIR CLERK.
MEMBERS CO-OPTED ON CORPORATION COMMITTEES.
CORPORATION CHIEF OFFICIALS AND STAFFS.
COMMITTEE OF GOVERNORS OF THE INGHAM INFIRMARY.
CHAMBER OF COMMERCE AND GROCERS ASSOCIATION.
COMMERCIAL TRAVELLERS' ASSOCIATION.
SOUTH SHIELDS MASTER BUILDERS ASSOCIATION.
GOSPEL TEMPERANCE UNION.
MASONIC LODGES OF THE BOROUGH.
HEAD TEACHERS AND STAFFS.
POSTMASTER AND STAFF.
MERCHANT SERVICE GUILD.
PERSONAL FRIENDS OF THE MAYOR.
REAR GUARD OF POLICE.
    The procession will leave Town Hall at 10-20 a.m.
Route.—Fowler Street, King Street, Market Place, and return
    by the same route.

    WILLIAM R. WILKIE, Chief Constable.

Chief Constable's Office,
12th November, 1933.

The guest list for Mayor's Sunday, 1933.

A series of images of the Mayor's Sunday Church Parade on 12th November 1933.

The Mayoress' reception, 29th November. This yearly reception was one of the highlights of the local municipal and social calendar and this photograph conveys only a little of the scale of the occasion. The Town Hall was said to resemble a vast conservatory with palms, foliage and rare lilies and orchids, many if not all the product of Shields' own municipal nurseries in the reception room. Music was supplied by the Zion Hall Unemployed Orchestra. Between the hours of three and five pm there was a continuous stream of callers.

Opening the Salvation Army Rainbow Fayre at the Havelock Citadel, 6th December. The girl is believed to be Eva Wilson and she is presenting a bouquet of bronze chrysanthemums to Mrs Lawlan. Also present was the town's MP, Mr Harcourt Johnson.

As Christmas approached the Lawlans were opening, attending and being guests of honour at schools, parties, sales of work and annual dinners. Christmas Day found them, with other members of the Public Assistance Committee, at the Ingham Infirmary where they toured the wards with carol singers. The Mayoress presenting every patient with a gift. Then they went to the Harton Institution. The *Gazette's* 'Plane Jane' was accompanying the party and from her account the wards were extensively decorated: 'the Female Chronic Infirm Ward adopting a Japanese theme, patients wearing Japanese caps and jackets and fluttering Japanese fans.' Another ward was christened lilac time and decorated entirely in lilac and yet another had adopted the 'Zuyder Zee' as its theme and was decorated with two huge windmills and masses of tulips. Christmas dinner for over 1,000 people was a huge undertaking: 'We went into the kitchens and watched the staff serving dinner with incredible speed and deftness. There were two enormous mountains of roast beef, already carved, and white-coated men were whacking out generous helpings on to every plate. Girls stood behind similar mountains of mashed potatoes and turnips, and as the plates came round they added big spoonfuls of these to the meat. Other girls stood waiting with huge jugs of gravy.'

On 12th January the Mayor attended a performance of *Babes in the Wood* at the Zion Hall Unemployed Recreational Centre in Laygate staged by unemployed men in aid of the Ingham Infirmary and the Shoeless Children's Fund. During a speech he apparently said that the unemployed should: 'get out and about and keep their eyes open for work. The Zion Hall was alright but you couldn't live on it.' The remark seems to have caused offence to the stewards who voted to write to Colonel R. Chapman and ask him to convey their unhappiness to the Mayor. One steward later remarked that the men who use the various unemployed recreational and occupational centres are, 'amongst the most vigorous and energetic seekers after work in Shields. If we were malingerers we would not be so keen to do voluntary labour. Mr Lawlan's remarks would be better directed at the men who are propping up the street corners and who go home to bed after signing on for their dole.'

A day or so later a Thomas Henderson remarked in the local press that it was the men on street corners who were really keeping their eyes open for work and it was the 'Zionites' who spent all day lounging over card tables.

On the evening of 9th March Mr Lawlan presided over what the following day's *Gazette* was to call: 'One the most extraordinary scenes of disorder ever witnessed in South Shields Council Chamber.' The Council had been discussing the appropriation of Harton Hospital by the Health Committee and the problems caused in finding beds for patients. Councillor Gompertz seems to have made derogatory remarks about Councillors Shearer and Chapman. Mayor Lawlan rebuked him: 'If you persist in this course the first thing I shall have to do is to clear out the public gallery then I shall deal with you. You are getting beyond bounds. You are no different from other members of this Council. Do not irritate me or you will find out … '

Gompertz: 'You did not take that attitude when Councillor Thompson called me a swine last night.'

The Mayor: 'I did not hear. I am very sorry but the people in the gallery will have to go.'

Gompertz: 'Come on we will go with the public.'

There were cries of 'Good old Gompy. Come to the Market.'

Empire Day, 24th May 1934. This is believed to be the West Park with the gentleman at the microphone being Lieut-Commander W. Carnall with Captain S. Blackwood and the Reverend R. Crossett. Around 450 boy scouts and cubs of the South Shields Scouts Association paraded at the West Park. Mr Lawlan spoke of the common bond of brotherhood that brought together men and women and children throughout the Empire. He said it was a family of around a quarter of a million people and comprised a great many different races who were united by mutual bonds into one great family. After the singing of the Doxology and the Benediction, the troops marched passed and saluted the Union Jack, the salute being taken by Colonel Wright.

What appears to be a great many Council Officials on their annual trip to Scarborough, 25th June. Included are: the Mayor and Mayoress, the Town Clerk, Mr H. Ayrey, and his wife and the Borough Treasurer, Mr R.H. Coulthard, and his wife.

At the North Foreshore for the opening of Harbour Drive, 27th June.

At the YMCA garden fete in the grounds of Undercliff at Cleadon village, 12th July. Mr Lawlan opened the fete. Also present were Sir James and Lady Readhead, Colonel and Mrs R. Chapman and Mr Alan Foster. The day before retiring as Mayoress, Mrs Mary Lawlan told the *Gazette* that every moment of the past year had been a delightful experience and remarked on the extraordinary number of women doing good behind the scenes for every church and every charity. She added that such work was also the enemy of loneliness, something that could easily afflict middle-aged women as their children grow up and leave the parental roof. On the day of her retirement she handed over a cheque for just over £600 to the Ingham Infirmary extension appeal, an organisation she had worked for and supported for much of her life.

Counting the collection. The occasion is unknown although this may also be a fundraising effort for the Infirmary. On 1st November 1937 Councillor Samuel Lawlan died suddenly at his home, Greystead in Grosvenor Road, he was 74. Obituaries appeared in the local and regional press over the following days and gave extensive coverage to his time at sea, war record and work with the town's public assistance and town improvement committees. His year as Mayor was mostly covered in one line.

Mayor Samuel Lawlan on the steps of the Town Hall.

YESTERDAY'S AND TODAY'S

The steel skeleton of the former Binns department store stands exposed during demolition. Here the outside stone work has been cropped level giving rise to rumours that part of the facade would be incorporated into the new building. Unfortunately this was not to be. The store closed on 1st July 1995 and demolition began in April 1997.

The interior and exterior of the former Barrington Street Baptist Church, date unknown. Churches and religious denominations have probably been in the town ever since there has been a town, although as with other institutions the line of descent can become hazy as it is traced back through the generations. Hodgson comments that there were Baptists in South Shields before and during

the 18th century. However, by 1768 their Chapel east of Laygate was in ruins. When it was later destroyed, presumably because of building work on the site, Nicholas Fairles notes that many human bones were dug up from the graveyard around it. Fairles saw the intact coffin of one of the ministers, and when it was opened the body was found to be prefect and the clothing quite fresh. After what seems to have been a very minimal presence in the town the movement began to grow from around 1818 when a young student preacher David Douglas was appointed to the town and on 25th April 1821 the foundation stone of the Barrington Street Church was laid.

There were some difficulties and disputes, the church was in debt and the first settled Pastor, the Reverend George Brown, did not stay settled for long. The next year he seceded with some of the congregation and formed the Particular Baptist Church. Another Pastor was appointed, but by 1827 the church appeared moribund. Its fortunes rose again in 1828 with the appointment of a Mr Dawson as Pastor and for some time around 1831 services were conducted by William Henry Angus who Hodgson calls: 'a truly remarkable Tynesider.' In 1832 Angus was preparing for a journey to help liquidate the chapel's debts when cholera broke out in Shields. That year, like many others who fought the disease's ravages, he succumbed and died from it himself. After 1841 the Reverend James Sneath largely, but not totally, reunited the town's Baptists around the Barrington Street with such success that debts of £620 were cleared and the congregation began to outgrow the building.

An early image of Westoe Road Baptist Church. The foundation stone was laid in April 1880, the building of red pressed brick and stone dressing in the free Italian style, opening in 1881.

Westoe Road Baptist Church interior, some time in the 1930s, decorated for a Sunday School anniversary.

Most churches have usually had a very active social and community side to them over the years. Although we are not experts in the matter it often seems from the evidence of old photographs that the 1920s and '30s were a time when a great deal of effort and thought was ploughed into these activities. Here an elaborate 'set' has been constructed in one of the churche's larger upstairs rooms for a bazaar.

Children taking part in a Christmas play at the church, December 1929. These Sunday School scholars were trained by Mrs Rene Grey.

A ladies sewing meeting at the church around 1929. A great number of useful items including many quilts were made during these occasion.

Members of the Westoe Baptist Church Sunday School, June 1945.

Akela leads the 5th South Shields Westoe Baptist Cub Scouts up Fowler Street after the Easter Procession held in the Market in 1963. The Church's Girl Guides follow behind.

Mrs Kirkwood and members of her Sunday school class, 1954. They are standing at the back of the church with part of Westoe Road visible behind them.

New members to the Church's Brownie pack in 1936.

Sunday Schools

Sunday schools have often been the stuff of happy memories, with group activities often making possible all kinds of activities that the individual would never be able to contemplate or afford on their own. Hodgson notes that there were Sunday schools in South Shields as early as 1807: 'The earliest Sunday school in connection with the free churches of which there is any record was established in 1810 in the long room of a public house in Pilot Street by a dissenting minister. In 1827 there were seven Sunday schools in the Borough, with 11,000 children in regular attendance. On 3rd June 1851, at a preliminary meeting in St John's Schoolroom, it was agreed that a Sunday school union should be formed in affiliation with the London Sunday School Union, its object being to stimulate and encourage the teachers already engaged in the work of religious instruction, to establish schools in various parts of the town, and to furnish Sunday school libraries etc. One feature of the union's work has been an annual parade and demonstration on Good Friday of the Sunday school children connected with the union which has become quite a feature in the town. The centenary of the establishment of Sunday schools by Robert Raikes was celebrated in the town on 23rd June 1880, by a great demonstration in which twenty-nine schools took part. Six thousand children assembled in the Market Place where a combined service of song was conducted by Thomas Lincoln, and a procession afterwards formed through the town.' Around 1900 there were 39 Sunday schools connected with the union with a total of 8,758 scholars and 900 teachers. There were ten Sunday schools attached to the various Episcopal churches in the Borough with a total attendance of 4,600 children exclusive of the two schools attached to the Harton Church, which had about 500 children in attendance.

Westoe Bridges

What is possibly the original Westoe Bridge. Initially there was just one section which spanned Westoe Road. The authors believe the girders were dated 1878 and were made by the Grange Iron Co of Durham.

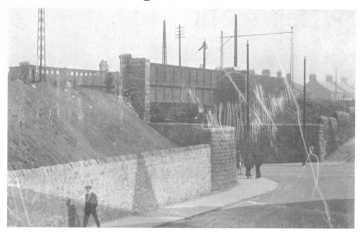

In 1874 the Whitburn Coal Company, an offshoot of the Harton Coal Company, had begun construction work on Whitburn Colliery and around the same time the bridge was erected as part of a four mile railway link between the colliery and the Deans area. The line's main traffic was an endless line of clanking coal wagons. In 1878 the construction of Westoe Lane Embankments caused this angry letter in the local press.

'Sir. I saw with pleasure the letter on the subject of the bridge and embankment in Westoe Lane. I cannot help expressing my astonishment, sir, at the want of respect that has been exhibited on the part of the majority of our town councillors for the feelings of our fellow townsmen in this instance. We had only one unobstructed entrance to our canny old town, and that has been recently much improved by being made wider, and having a flagged footpath on both sides, and now we have the unspeakable mortification of seeing one of the most unsightly structures erected across it with its more abominable embankments attached to either side, thus separating the old town from the new. One argument advanced in favour of this piece of jobbery was that this is not a residential borough. It is very true, sir, that we are not a community of Lords and Dukes, but we are a people numbering over 50,000 men, women and children, with thoughts, feelings, tastes and appetites common to our race, and we are capable of appreciating the beauties of nature of which a well arranged park would afford, be it public or private quite as well as either Lords, Dukes, retired tradesmen or merchants whichever were in the mind of the speaker when he said that this is not a residential borough. I give it as my opinion that we have more than enough to contend with already; what with ballast hills, level crossings, and badly arranged streets, without being insulted and annoyed by this new obstruction. The colliery company are able to pay for such accommodation as they require, and it is clearly the duty of our representatives to preserve us from this last encroachment upon this fairest portion of our town. I hope, sir, the people will allow by their actions in November what they think of this business. After they have done all they can I hope they will hold a meeting and denounce the men who have taken part in this most disgraceful proceedings, and then call upon them to resign.

Yours, A Native

In the early 1920s something was done about the problem. The Westoe Lane Bridge Improvement Scheme turned Westoe Bridge into Westoe Bridges. An extra span was added so Imeary Street could run directly on to Westoe Road. This view is shortly before the work was declared complete by the Mayor, Alderman J.G. Winskill on 12th May 1925. The contractor was Gustavus Baily and Co Ltd. Dignitaries were treated to lunch at the Golden Lion.

The demolition of Westoe Bridges Imeary Street section on 16th October 1994 following the closure of Westoe Colliery. The section over Westoe Road was taken down a week later on the 23rd.

The Wouldhave Memorial

Above left: The less favoured of the two top designs for the Wouldhave and Greathead Lifeboat Memorial. *Above right*: The memorial under construction. Hodgson writes that the memorial was first suggested in 1887 by the then Mayor Alderman Eltringham. There seems to have been a lively debate in the town about both the exact origins of the lifeboat and how far the monument should be a commemoration of Wouldhave and or Greathead and or Queen Victoria's Jubilee. A competition was launched in connection with the design of the memorial and some of the conditions being: 'designs to include plans, elevations, section specification, and an estimate of the total cost. The drawings to be in outline only, and to a scale of four feet to one inch. The total cost, including the architect's commission of 5%, may not exceed the sum of £500. The committee do not bind themselves to carry out any of the designs. In the event of them not doing so, a premium of ten guineas will be awarded.' The winning design was by a Mr J.H Morton, architect of South Shields. Messrs Stout and Dockwray, also architects of South Shields, were second. Part of the winning submission reads: 'In preparing my design it will be noticed I have assumed the site of the said memorial be on the approach to the pier promenades, in the centre of the carriage road and facing the Marine Park's restaurant. The first stage would be utilised as a fountain. On the side facing the approach from the town will be a tablet bearing an inscription to be decided by the committee. Dog troughs are shown round the outside of the basin. The second stage would contain a large medallion of Wouldhave surrounded by a laurel wreath and having a model of the lifeboat below. On the north tablet will be a representation of the building of the lifeboat by Greathead and on the south the saving of a shipwrecked crew.'

The memorial was unveiled by Alderman Eltringham on the occasion of the opening of the Marine Parks, 25th June 1890.

A postcard view of the *Tyne* lifeboat and the memorial. This is unusual in that the memorial is seen from the easterly direction looking towards the junction of Ocean Road/Sea View Terrace.

The monument after the attack of Thursday, 2nd October 1941.

The monument in winter, *circa* 1960.

An architect's drawing of the Police Station in Kepple Street. As they were being erected around 1892 a contemporary journalist enthused: 'At the foot of Russell Street and just beyond the post office on the site of the old Phoenix Glass Works and in a hollow close to the railway, the new police buildings are at present in the course of completion. They will present a somewhat imposing and varied front, much of which will be hidden by other buildings. However, placed in a more central and accessible situation the new police buildings would have ranked high among the architectural features of the borough.' The building cost around £22,000 and was official opened by Mayor Alderman J. Rennoldson on 6th June 1893.

The station seen behind the rubble generated by the demolition of Binns department store in April 1997.

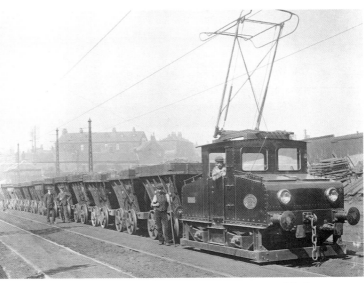

Harton Coal Company Electric locomotive E2. Windmill Hill is at the back of the picture. The locomotive was ordered from Siemens Brothers Dynamo Works Ltd of Stafford in 1908 although most of the parts are believed to have been made in Munich, Germany. Delivery to the HCC took place in 1909. The locomotive worked in Shields until 1984 when it was withdrawn and sold for scrap by the NCB. An eleventh hour deal led to it being bought for preservation by the West Yorkshire Transport Museum and transported to Bradford. In 1989 it was sold again and moved to Halifax. Then in 1991 it was bought by Beamish Open Air Museum.

The locomotive in storage at Beamish Open Air Museum at the back of the Foulbridge tramcar depot. There are plans to restore the locomotive to working order as a maintenance vehicle. However, its identical twin, E10, is now in the process of restoration at the Tanfield Railway in Gateshead and may soon be running under its own power.

The unveiling of the Queen Victoria statue at the Town Hall, 7th May 1913. A public meeting held on 16th May 1901 decided to erect a statue to the Queen. In February 1908, or thereabouts, the decision was made to invite a Mr Toft of London and a Mr Doyle of Hartlepool to submit designs for a statue. In February 1911 Mr Toft was selected. His design was for a standing figure of Victoria at a cost of £1,000. For the unveiling the forecourt was barried off and the area immediately around the statue was reserved for ticket holders. Near the Town Hall steps were a number of men from the 4th Howitzers, the 7th Durhams, National Reservists and Territorials. The statue was unveiled by Sir Hedworth Williamson of Whitburn Hall.

Under wraps. The Queen Victoria statue at Chichester ready to be transported for restoration. The statue had been moved to Chichester ostensibly to allow road widening at the Town Hall forecourt in spite of public protest and suggestions that Caldwell roundabout would be a far better place for it. Little care seems to have been given to the statue once it reached Chichester. The authors remember passing it on the No 7 bus and seeing it encrusted with soot and bird droppings. When the proposed Chichester Metro station made it impossible for the statue to stay where it was, the decision was made to return it to the Town Hall forecourt.

One of Queen Victoria's companions, or the Town Hall Hussies as they are also known. While researching these pages we found plenty of information on the Victoria statue, but not so much on the ladies. They are actually lamp standards made of cast iron and each cost just over £71 and were painted to represent bronze. Mounted on royal blue granite pedestals, the three veiled ones are emblematic of night, the unveiled ones being emblematic of day. The statue pedestals were also interconnected by cast iron chains. However, we don't know who designed them. It may well have been Albert Toft but we would welcome further information.

The statues were later relocated to the South Marine Park. One of them is seen here. Two were returned to the Town Hall forecourt alongside Victoria in 1983. Time capsules were apparently buried under them containing two Catherine Cookson books, a holiday guide to South Tyneside and a Scott Dobson Geordie passport. Here Florence Archer (now Swann) poses alongside one of the statues in the early 1960s.

The courtyard of the South Shields Gas Company's stables and garage near the Town Hall, *circa* 1920.

The year 2000 and the refurbished buildings are now part of a group of industrial/business units.

The Marsden Limestone Quarries, *circa* 1895. The exact location is difficult to place, however, Lizzard Lane may run left to right.

Part of the then redundant limestone quarries in use as a motorcycle track, *circa* 1961. This seems to be the section to the west of Lizard Lane.

Construction work underway on the Metro line, *circa* 1980. The route from Heworth to Shields was for many years a 'now its on, now its off' project as various cash crisis and cutbacks hit the system. The line under construction in the foreground was not actually the Metro line but was to connect Westoe Colliery to the British Rail network.

Around twenty years later and a few hundred yards nearer to Tyne Dock a Metro train about to run under West Park Road bridge. The line to Westoe has now gone. The train is actually a rarity, three cars instead of the usual one or two and was on a special express service taking people home from the 1999 Great North Run. The service had been introduced following complaints that the normal service couldn't cope with the amount of runners returning home from Shields.

TOWN IMPROVEMENTS

What is believed to be the official opening of the Coast Road by Herbert Morrison MP, Minister of Transport, on the 2nd November 1929. The following is from the programme of events:

'On arrival at Mowbray Road, the South Shields terminus of the Coast Road, His Worship the Mayor of South Shields (Alderman J. Dunlop) will invite the Minister to perform the opening ceremony. The Borough Engineer and Surveyor of South Shields will thereupon present the Minister with a pair of scissors for the purpose of cutting the tape across the road on the west side of the island. The Minister will then cut the tape. Simultaneously the Mayor of South Shields will cut the tape on the east side of the island (a pair of scissors being presented to him by the Borough Engineer and Surveyor of South Shields for the purpose). After the tapes have been cut the Minister will declare the road open for public use. The Minister with the party assembled will then proceed along the road to the terminus of the Coast Road on the south side of the Lighthouse Bridge, where it joins the road in continuation called Mill Lane, which has been widened and reconstructed by South Shields Rural District Council. A tape will be stretched across the road at this point, and the Chairman of the South Shields Rural District Council (Councillor R. Hann) will invite the Minister to open the road. The Surveyor of the Rural District Council will present the Chairman with a pair of scissors. The Minister and the Chairman will cut the tape and the Minister declare the road open for public use. The party will return via Whitburn, Cleadon and Harton to the Town Hall at South Shields. (The three pair of scissors are being provided by the British Reinforced Concrete Engineering Co Ltd.)'

Above and opposite page top: A panoramic view of South Shields Gas Works. We believe this is a composite image and may not be entirely accurate. Reputedly extra buildings were sometimes added to such photographs to make the plant look more impressive. The date is before the company's centenary in 1924 and likely after major rebuilding work in 1901. As this chapter notes, South Shields Corporation has been responsible for many improvements in the town although gas was introduced long before the Corporation's formation in 1850. Experiments in coal gas street lighting, 'lighting by smoke', took place in Pall Mall, London, in 1807 with the first statutory gas company the Gas Light and Coke Company beginning operations five years later. In December 1823 circulars were apparently sent out to around 350 South Shields' inhabitants by local tradesmen inviting the recipients to a meeting at Oyston's, the Golden Lion Hotel. The signatories on the circular included: Edward Pattison, hardware-man; James Kirkley, linen draper; John Allen; John Waller; William Anderson, timber merchant; Joseph Hargrave, grocer; Relph Middlemost; William Richardson, linen draper; Timothy Matterson; Thomas Wilson, shipowner and Benjamin Fenwick, woollen draper. Records of the company are scarce, but the authors believe the meeting was held on either 5th or 9th December 1823 and was chaired by William Chapman. It was decided capital of £4,000 would be needed to set up a gas company and that revenue of £600 a year might be obtained. Hodgson notes that the South Shields Gas Company was formed by deed of covenant dated 17th March 1824 with a capital of £4,000 in £25 shares. The first works were constructed in what was called, 'Paradise' on the south side of the Mill Dam. St Hilda Pit was located nearby, coal extraction began there in 1825. Both pit and gas works were likely to be a source of 'synergy', as the jargon is today. At least one person, William Anderson, having interests in both concerns.

Gas was first supplied to houses and shops in the town on 1st October 1824. Five years later, on 1st November 1829, the Town Commissioners lighted part

of the town with gas, twenty lamps being provided for the purpose. The cost of the public lighting at this period is recorded to have been at the rate of £2 5s per lamp for the six winter months; it being the practice not to light the lamps for seven nights at the time of the full moon. In the year 1845 the number of public gas lamps had increased to 178. There is at least some suggestion of monopoly pricing, with at least two rival companies being formed then abandoned as the South Shields Gas Company agreed to reduce its prices. The 1853 Town Improvement Act empowered the Corporation to spend £10,000 acquiring the company, but by then the company was worth considerably more and the purchase did not take place. In 1855 the company was reorganised, the works reconstructed and extended and the gas mains reached Tyne Dock. Around 1864, South Shields Gas Company seems to have acquired the Jarrow Gas Company. It extensively rebuilt and enlarged the Jarrow plant in 1876, and again in 1913, and used it to supply Hebburn and the Boldons. In 1879 the company was authorised by Parliament to supply gas to Whitburn, but the 'standard' price of gas was fixed at 3s 3d and dividends limited to a maximum of 7%. Along with other extensive projects, such as the building of a coast road and a new Town Hall, a Town Improvement Bill of 1878

Part of the gas works retort house interior.

would have given the Corporation the power to buy the gas company. However, the bill failed in January 1879 and the company remained in private hands. Extensive reconstruction and extension work took place in around 1879 with the new works being opened on 10th February 1880. Yet more large extensions took place in 1901-2 including a new mechanised retort house. In that year 400 million cubic feet of gas was sold for domestic use and a dividend of 7³/₄% was paid on ordinary stock. In 1896 the Corporation's electric power station went on line, undoubtedly this would be seen as a rival by the company, as previously the Corporation had lobbyed Parliament to restrict the company's prices. In 1889 the company introduced the eight hours shift system for stokers and other staff. In 1900 the prepayment meter system was introduced and proved to be very popular with consumers. During 1909 the company opened showrooms at South Shields and Jarrow for the exhibition of gas apparatus and other useful gas appliances. During the First World War many employees joined the forces and female labour was introduced, 'wherever possible'. Public lighting was abolished and lighting restrictions imposed upon the public. In 1920 the Gas Regulation Act required the company to sell gas by the 'Therm' rather than volume. While around this time many people were becoming aware of the advantages of electric lighting, with residents clamouring for electric street lighting, the two methods seem to have co-existed in some form for many years. A 1936 report suggests that in that year the Corporation maintained 1,865 gas lamps alongside 1,412 electric lights.

The company's registered offices at Chapter Row.

Over the centuries there have been almost endless schemes to improve the town. Chronicling what often seems like endless battles, fought on many fronts and with a constantly changing cast of protagonists would be a huge undertaking. The struggle to improve South Shields has been entwined with that to improve the River Tyne and wrest control of affairs from Newcastle and other bodies. There have also been competing and conflicting interests and very different views on the best way of moving forwards inside the town. This section is not even an attempt to sketch the outline of town improvements, but just to supply a little information. Hodgson notes that there were attempts to obtain Acts of Parliament for 'paving, lighting and watching the town' in 1810 and again in 1815. In 1828, 'when the town contained over 17,000 inhabitants, and had a dozen shipyards in active employment in addition to the glass and chemical works,' another such bill was approved on 24th September at a public meeting in the Town Hall. It proposed that the government of the town be placed in the hands of a body of Commissioners, which included all Justices of the Peace residing in South Shields and Westoe and every person who in his own right, or right of his wife, possessed a certain level of property.

Among the Commissioners' responsibilities were streets and highways and the police force. The Commissioners also had the power to levy a rate not exceeding 8d in the pound (in old money) on the value of agricultural land, docks, shipyards, manufactories and other property. Hodgson notes another group of citizens, who seemed to include owners of manufactories and other properties, immediately convened another meeting to oppose the bill on the grounds that it would lead to an unnecessary tax in times of reduced trade. They failed, and the bill later became law. Despite their limited powers and resources the Commissioners were able to make some improvements to the town. At one point they seem to have instituted a scheme where paupers in the Poor House were paid three shillings a week in addition to the amount they received in relief to work as labourers and scavengers. There are suggestions this scheme was not always popular amongst those normally employed as labourers and scavengers as well as the paupers themselves.

South Shields was granted its Charter of Incorporation as a Borough in September 1850. The new Corporation began reorganising the police force, increasing the number employed to fourteen and investigating ways of improving the water supply, which, Hodgson notes, was then still in the hands of the old South Shields Water Company. At that time the company was supplementing the supply obtained from Caldwell and the Dean Burn by pumping from the Pigeon Well into a high tower which stood in the yard at St Hilda Colliery. It was also collecting water from Westoe Lane Well into a reservoir near Westoe Lane which was unfortunately 'in a most disgusting condition polluted by vegetable matter and animal filth.'

General progress may have been slow. An 1855 *Shields Gazette* editorial complained that little improvement was really happening under the new regime. Here the *Gazette* responds to the Mayor's remark that although the council had not done much, what they had done they had done effectively: 'We trust the Mayor and his supporters will consider that if they go on doing so little, and that little so effectively, the whole of the present generation will be dead before their sanitary condition is improved. The worst saved public money is that which is saved from the cause of public cleanliness and health. The best method of managing the "limited finances" of a town like South Shields is to spend at once the whole sum required in order to place it under good sanitary conditions and to call upon the public to pay it off according to the plans familiar to all the Public Health Bills. It is not for want of money but for want of thorough conviction of the value of public health measures, joined in the case of some, to more sordid motions, which prevents the promptest and speediest possible application of sanitary work to all towns.'

As well as the general unsanitary state of much of Shields, another consideration was the arrival of infectious diseases by sea. Cholera had raged through the town in 1831 and 1848 and on several other occasions. Hodgson noted that it seems to have taken the smallpox epidemic of 1871 to spur the Corporation into a real and determined effort to grapple with the unsanitary state of the town. The first smallpox case appears to have been discovered on 10th October 1870 when a travelling showman who applied for admission to the Workhouse Hospital was discovered to be in a virulent state. He survived and, through isolating him, the infection was contained. However, on Sunday 20th November a seaman reached his home on Swan's Bank, Johnson's Hill, and three days later symptoms of smallpox appeared. The disease spread through that densely populated area very quickly. An account, which we have been unable to source suggested the occupants of the house were aware the man had smallpox when they took him in. The account also described the disease's spread: 'Soon the neighbouring air became contaminated with various poison, members of families in West Holborn district were suddenly stricken with the malady and the epidemic spread of the contagion was assisted by the persistence with which women of the poorer classes visit the houses of their suffering neighbours, although they can do no good, risking the lives of themselves and their families.'

Further cases of infection kept on arriving in the town. A seaman from an Italian barque died in Tyne Dock Station waiting room only a matter of hours after landing. Hodgson notes that every precaution possible against the disease's spread was taken although other sources suggest that many officials were slow to react to the disease's progress while it was still in the poorer areas of the town: 'Many lives would undoubtedly have been spared and much misery prevented had not a contemptible squabbling as to whose duty it was to see the Vaccination Act enforced broken out and precluded, to a great extent, anticipatory means (of checking the disease). Knowing, as everyone does, the numerous agencies by which the contagions may be transmitted – that it may traverse the air to a wide extent – that it may be communicated by clothing – and that a healthy person may inhale the poison by contact with one in whom the disease is in its initial stage – we are surprised at the indifference with which for a time the people of South Shields generally regarded the rapid development in their midst of perhaps the most contagious of diseases, no less than at which the Guardians of the Poor did the little which they seemed to think was necessary to arrest its progress.'

The epidemic raged until the June of 1871 with 4,000 known cases of infection and the number of known deaths being 373. As a result of the epidemic the Corporation created a separate sanitary department with a staff of horses and men to do the scavenging work of the town directly, and some work was done on clearing slums. The first Borough Medical Officer was appointed in 1874, Hodgson notes that this was only done after much discussion and delay. He was a Dr John Spear of Wigan and shortly after his appointment he began to institute a system for the inspection of shipping for disease and the old ferry boat *Durham* was converted for use as a hospital ship. Dr Spear is reported as describing the existing smallpox hospital as being 'little better than a shed' and in 1877 the Council purchased land in Dean Lane for what was to have been a building with two pavilion wards. However, it was not until 1882 that the Corporation set about erecting the Deans Hospital with accommodation for thirty-four patients. It opened on 9th May 1883 and the Corporation made it free to all townspeople.

A postcard of Ralph Wright, boot and shoemakers which we believe was located just off Ocean Road. Around the end of the 19th century the state of the drainage in the area was causing some concern to local residents as this letter to the *Gazette* testifies:

Sir. It is not necessary for the residents of Ocean Road to go to Cumberland to see a lake, for whenever it rains rather heavily they get one at their own doors. Our lake has the dead wall of the workhouse on one side, and that architectural adornment (according to the town surveyor) the skating rink, and homes of the usual Shields style on the other. Yesterday afternoon it rained heavily for about fifteen minutes, and in that time Ocean Road was flooded for about 120 yards, and opposite Shortridge Street the water rose fifteen inches in that time, the two drains having got stopped with the earthy matter which came down with the flood from the unpaved streets behind Dale Street. Before the large sewer was put in Ocean Road our lake used to appear with nearly every shower of rain, and I have seen it appear and disappear three times in twenty-four hours, and we fondly hoped that since we had got the large drain that our lake would have been seen no more. But alas! It returned again yesterday, and in greater depth than ever, and if it had continued raining for another quarter of an hour several of the homes in Ocean Road and Dale Street would have been flooded. The reason for these periodic floods is this, there are only three drains in Ocean Road from the Marine School to Seafield Terrace. There ought to be eight more. Why this was not done when the large sewer was put in 'no fellah can understand'. Next time a lake is ordered we humbly suggest that it be located outside the aristocratic houses of Sea View, or Wellington or Ogle Terraces, so that a lake composed of Shields rainwater may be properly appreciated, or better still, let a talkative Councillor, wise Alderman, or even the town surveyor come and live next door to the beautiful skating rink, and then we will be able to contemplate the beauties of the Ocean Road lake district! We do not expect any redress from our miss-called Town Improvement Committee, especially after they have allowed such ludicrous mistakes as have made the Bath Street Estate the laughing stock of the town. We simply want to protest through the medium of your columns against the recurrence of the Ocean Road lake.

Yours truly, Ocean Roaders

South Shields Council workmen loading a lorry with an excavator, *circa* 1950. The location is unknown, though we suspect the Tyne is below the horizon and this is the removal of a section of a ballast hill. The amount of ships' ballast dumped in the town has been phenomenal and has influenced much of the landscape.

A general clearance work around River Drive, *circa* 1952. The area to the right is now occupied by Cookson Court.

The Ingham Infirmary. According to Hodgson: 'The building cost £6,815 exclusive of furnishings and is in a modified style of Queen Ann architecture. The deed of the trust which built the infirmary specified that the institution was to be used for ever for the sick and lame poor residing or being in the borough of South Shields and the surrounding district. During the first year, 546 patients were admitted of whom 95 were in-patients. A total of 3,695 casualties were also treated.'

Harton Cemetery. Opened in February 1891, Hodgson notes: 'The cemetery is probably one of the handsomest and most tastefully laid out in the north being approached from the highway by a broad avenue. The entrance gateway, superintendent's house and chapels are in the late decorated Gothic style, the chapels being connected by an open archway over which there is a graceful spire rising to a height of 103 feet.'

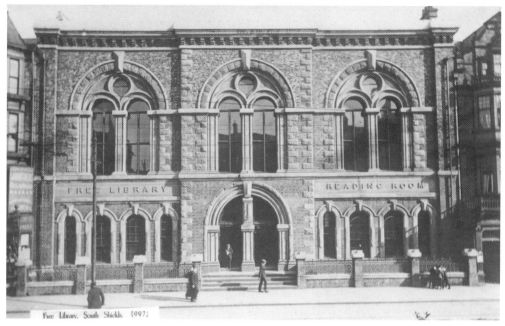

Free Library, South Shields (997)

A Monarch postcard featuring the unmistakable facade of the 'Old Library' building in Ocean Road. Over the years there have been many changes to the structure and function of the building. After the opening of the Central Library in Prince Georg Square this building seemed to be without a clear use but has now become a town museum and an exhibition on the life of Catherine Cookson. When she was nothing but a young girl from Leam Lane she would have been amazed to think half the ground floor would later be given over to an exhibition on her life! Hodgson notes that the earliest recorded public reading institution was the Lawe Newsroom founded on 20th February 1788, the location of which appears uncertain. The society seems to have been a sort of shipowners' club and had some involvement with the construction of the lifeboat. It was dissolved in 1802 and a newsroom was established in the old Town Hall. This was itself dissolved in 1855 when the Corporation moved into the building. The South Shields Literary, Mechanical and Scientific Institution was formed in 1825 and, Hodgson notes, by the end of its first year it had nearly 200 members and 400 volumes. The institute prospered and various offshoots were formed including the debating group, the Dialectical Society. The institute was re-opened as a public library by the Mayor, Alderman Terrot Glover on 15th October 1873. For some time the upper floor was used as a meeting room, but around 1888 the library had outgrown the ground floor and the reference library and museum were transferred upstairs while the whole of the ground floor was given over to circulating stock.

The bowling green at the West Park. We believe Shields Council was initially unwilling to provide this park due to their expenditure on the Marine Parks. However, pressure from residents apparently made them change their minds.

Marsden Road Aged Miners' Homes. They were officially opened in 1915 and early residents presumably found themselves in almost a self-contained community as Marsden Road would be little more than a rough track. It would be interesting to know the utilities initially provided and how residents maintained contact with their relatives who were presumably in Shields. They must have found the building of the Co-op shop across the road and the arrival of the Economic bus service quite a blessing.

Four of James Cleet's photographs of 'problem' areas in South Shields. They are believed to show the Adelaide Street area. The images are dated January 1938. Joyce Carlson recalls the area:

'My mother's cousin, Florrie, lived in the area. There were just two rooms and a small scullery with no window, it was pitch black. She had three children and her old father was permanently in the brass bedstead in the living room. He had a long grey beard and striped pyjamas. He was a very nice man and they were a very nice family. The rest of the family would sleep on what were called desk beds. They were like a small wardrobe, but when you opened the door a bed folded out instead. I think the children all slept in them. Unfortunately, the house always seemed damp and confined. Florrie used to show us the wallpaper lifting of the wall with the dampness. Very often, when I was sitting, a bug would drop on my shoulder either from the ceiling or the wall. They had four families to one yard with one toilet and no running water. My aunt was looking forwards to getting a council house so she could move out, but the war started and council house building stopped so they had to stay on.'

Members of Harton Parish Council. The Council strenuously opposed the efforts of South Shields to incorporate Harton into Shields. While Shields claimed incorporation would mean that villages could enjoy the amenities of Shields, such as its parks and libraries as a right, Harton Councillors claimed Shields only wanted Harton because of the financial contribution Harton householders would then be forced to make to the coffers of the South Shields Corporation.

Harton village, *circa* 1914.

Some of the more expensive housing in the Harton area – Grange Avenue
(*above*) and Linden Gardens (*below*). We suspect the date of both is around
1910. We imagine that many of these residents would not be too happy with
South Shields Council's stated idea of housing former slum area dwellers in
new council-built properties around the Harton District, principally in the new
Cleadon Park Estate. Perhaps they need not have worried. There are plenty of
claims that Cleadon Park rents were fixed high enough to deter many poorer
Shields folk and that houses were often allocated to Councillors and council
employees who were wealthy enough to employ servants to clean and cook in
their new houses.

Perhaps one of the first signs that Harton was under new management was the construction of the Cleadon tramway and King George Road. For this 1923 view the photographer seems to have been standing in the centre of what is now Caldwell Roundabout. St Peter's Church is to the left. On the original image it is possible to make out what seems to be the construction of houses to the right of the church.

Harton village from what is now King George Road. The small railway visible is likely to be a contractor's line.

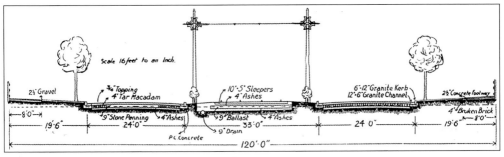

A sectional plan of King George Road.

House construction underway. We believe this is in the Central Avenue area, although are unsure of the exact date and location.

A mid 1930s advert for the type of new private housing then springing up around the Harton Caldwell area. The young couple look idyllic and for many people these new private estates would have been accommodation they could only have dreamed of moving into a few years before. Only a few years later, many would find their dreams in ruins with wartime bombing reducing swathes of these estates to rubble.

South Shield's own supertram, No 52, in the Dean Road depot. The car was assembled at the depot in 1936, the year the bulk of the tram routes were converted to trolleybus operation. With the closure of the last tram route in 1946 it was purchased by Sunderland Corporation.

Interior shots of the entrance and stairway, the saloon and the top deck of No 52. The inside of the car was described by a contemporary tramway journal:

'The tramcar body, built by the Brush Electrical Engineering Co Ltd, has seating for 60 passengers. Entrance is effected by means of a wide centre doorway, the doors themselves combine special sliding and folding arrangements. Ventilation in each saloon is by means of three half drop windows, in the upper, six extractor ventilators are fitted in the ceiling panels with stainless steel grids. The seats are arranged traversley with reversible backs. Those in the lower saloon being upholstered in an attractive patterned Moquette, bordered and panelled with brown leather, whilst the seats in the upper are upholstered in red leather. A notable feature of the upper saloon is the curved plate glass panels on each side of the roof to facilitate better lighting and give improved visibility for the passengers riding on the top deck. The electric lighting is decorative and efficient, being provided by semi-concealed continuous panels of glazed moonstone glass in chromium plated frames. The general air of brightness is reinforced by polished stainless steel stair-rails and interior fittings. The tramcar undoubtedly represents a distinct step forwards in exterior design. It has already met with a cordial reception from the travelling public in South Shields, where the citizens are perhaps the most trammed in Great Britain, with the possible exception of Sunderland.'

Local comedians, Tommy Duffy (Alan Fox)
and Allan Snell.

Acknowledgements

The following people have been involved in the production of this book:

Geordie Atkinson, Keith Bardwell, David Barnsley, Paul Barrett, Ron Bell, Tom Best, Dennis Boad, Fred Bond, Kathleen Burdon, Ken Corner, David Charlton, Ron Davison, Thomas Dodds Johns, Harry Fitzsimmons, Tommy Duffy (Alan Fox), Irene Foster, Richard Fox, Mary Gibbs, John Gordon, Muriel Hanson, Frank Heywood, Peter Headly, Roland 'Rolley' Headly, Doris Johnson, John Johnson, Derrick Knott, everyone at Westoe Baptist Church and its predecessors, Justine Lenney, Joan Mullen, Margaret Pickering, Eddie Post, George Post, Mr Purvis (The Pilot), Joyce Roberts, Mrs Bone, Mary McNeaney, Alan Packer, Dallas Park, Irene Spence, Stuart Smith, Thelma Small (née Taws), Eva Todd, Flo Thornborrow, Neil Tweddell, Sheila Tweddell, Stan Tweddell, Robert Wray and everyone at the Archives of Beamish Museum.

South Tyneside Libraries
The Shields Gazette
Beamish, the North of England Open Air Museum
George Nairn
John Johnson/Ken Groundwater Collection (back cover and inside)

As these acknowledgements were put together very quickly we are sure to have missed some names out, so let us know and we will put you in the next one.

Special mention for Matthew Barrett, Pauline Chiu, Paul Mabley, Jaswinda Sing Puna, Steve Charlton and the rest of CBIS 1999-2000.

Additionally thanks are due to Dennis Boad and Robert Wray for additional research and proof reading.

Special mention for the South Shields Sandancers World Wide Web page.